*How to Make Money
with Your Crafts*

Linda Henderson
Jan. 14, 1978

Leta W. Clark

How to Make Money with Your Crafts

WILLIAM MORROW & COMPANY, INC.
NEW YORK 1973

Printed in the United States of America.

Library of Congress Catalog Card Number 73-15308

1 2 3 4 5 78 77 76 75 74

ISBN 0-688-00225-0
ISBN 0-688-05225-8 (pbk.)

To Cath, Mills and Caroline,
in the order of their appearance

ACKNOWLEDGMENTS

It would be impossible to thank all the people who gave so generously of their thinking, their time and their contacts to make this book a reality. Help was extended on corporate and on personal levels in what seemed to me to be unprecedented amounts, for which I am very grateful. My sincere appreciation to you all, with special applause for Elaine Markson and Milton E. Maybruck.

Contents

Introduction

There are many reasons why I decided to write this book. Some are obvious, impersonal business facts that indicated to me that the time was right for such a guidebook. Other reasons are retrospectively personal, because I remember back to the days when I first opened my own business and see how the many blunders I made could have been avoided or at least lessened. The other reasons are somewhat philosophical, having to do with my attitude toward one's work and one's career.

The law of supply and demand weaves in and out of the business facts that made me start to write. Toward the end of the 1950s and in the beginning of the 1960s many Americans underwent a change in their attitudes and life styles. The conformity of the 50s, with its compartmentalized rigidities of the "right address," the "right clothes," the "right job" was giving way to a freer way of living. People stopped trying to look or behave exactly like other people and began to feel that it was all right just to look like themselves and act like themselves and feel like themselves.

1

The phrase "Do your own thing" began to crop up, a phrase that could not have been part of the language five years earlier. The sacred cows lost credibility and buying patterns that had been so firmly established began to waver. The European couture, designer originals, styles decreed and promoted by leading fashion stores and publications began to lose impact as a sizable number of Americans started to search out and buy fashions and home furnishings to please themselves that were *not* necessarily "in fashion."

The very young were most outspoken in their disavowal of styles that spelled conformity. The hippie, flower-child nonconformists dressed and lived as far away as they could from the upwardly mobile, status-conscious citizen of the 1950s. In womenswear, fashion began to come up from almost anyplace—the past, the street, the imaginations of designers not related to any one general trend. Some of it was flashy, sensational, and cheap enough to be almost disposable after a few wearings. But it kicked the habit of big mass production. Some of these small businesses stuck, they survived. Concurrently, life styles focused on a return to the land and ecology became a national concern. Handmade and homemade items increased in favor and some of their mass-produced counterparts began to lose sales.

This presented a problem to American merchants, used to sure-selling duplicates of French couture fashions or large, feature-packed cars whose names alone indicated the owner's economic status. Home-sewing, hand-knitting, crocheting and art-needlework sales zoomed, as did gourmet cookery equipment.

Department-store executives became aware of the "little boutiques" that seemed to have sprung up overnight, stocked with one-of-a-kind items often created by the store owner. The boutiques' prices were high, but the stock was unique and customers flocked in, suddenly willing to take a chance on the rightness of merchandise that did not have the correct big-store label on it.

Far-seeing retailers began to seek out small manufacturers, designers, and craftspeople who could furnish unique quality products for newly set-up boutique corners within the big store, in an attempt to bring the customers back into their former dependency. The idea was fine; the results were often chaotic. Retailers, used to dealing with the giants of mass production, assumed that the new resources understood the stores' methods of operation. The small designer and craftsperson, on the other hand, usually didn't have the foggiest idea of the mass-marketing operation and often didn't care. Sales were sometimes made under the most amazing circumstances. It was a good time to be a small designer or craftsperson, but a bad time to be a department-store buyer.

Obviously no economic process is this simple—many other factors contributed to the change in the American way of living. But the simple ratio of supply and demand brought us into the 1970s with a relatively small supply of quality boutique designers and craftspeople and a rather large demand for unique hand-crafted goods. Meanwhile, an interest in do-it-yourself crafts had continued to grow. Instructions, courses, craft shops, books, and magazines had flooded the market with information, all telling the consumer how simple yet how satisfying it is to work with one's own hands. The consumer bought and worked. So, hovering in the wings were scores of skilled nonprofessionals whose craft hobbies stretched back over the previous ten years and whose work was sometimes of outstanding caliber.

One of my reasons for writing this book is to help this nonprofessional bridge the gap between hobby and business, a gap that is often as emotional as it is informational. I was one of the "little" designers selling to boutiques and boutique shops in department stores at the end of the 1950s and the beginning of the 1960s. Before the end of the decade I had returned to the marketing and sales promotion work that had been my career prior to designing. So to many people in the market I still offer that magic combination of both a designing and a merchandising background.

Rarely has a month gone by in which I have not received at least one phone call from an acquaintance who has a friend/wife/sister/parent/child who makes marvelous hats/sweaters/pillows/rugs that are really just as good as those at Bendel's/Bonwit's/Bloomingdale's. Would I please suggest a few ways the creator of said product could get in to see a buyer and sell a few numbers?

Sure, I say, but seeing a buyer is the last step. Has the person checked the market to be sure the product is competitive, professional, really keyed to those stores? How about costing the item realistically? And firm, true delivery time promises—have they been worked out by the dozen in case an order is placed? Usually the phone call ends there. Occasionally, the nonprofessional has done enough background work and then I am happy to help if I can.

The background work is not mysterious. It is the normal preparation the professional makes before showing a line to a buyer. With it, the way is paved for profitable sales. Without it, the way is perilous. When I first started designing I knew very little about setting up a small business, keeping books, making out invoices, terms, costing and dealing with sewing machine operators, sales agents and contractors. Fortunately, through my promotion background, I knew the fabric markets, how to spot trends, and the marketing cycles for the fashion and home-furnishings industries. So I made all the right things—but lost a lot of money until I picked up the information I was lacking.

About two years ago I began to sort out the marketing information I had accumulated during the brief years I was designing, comparing it with friends who have been or still are designing. We seemed to agree that the information is highly communicable. A new designer would have an easier first year, with a higher chance of success, if the basics were learned before a buyer placed the initial order.

I organized what I considered to be the basics and began teaching seminars to skilled nonprofessionals who wanted to sell their handicrafts. The overwhelming response to the classes, both from the students and from the industry, confirmed my theory that the industry *is* diligently searching out new designers, while at the same time the new designers-to-be are trying to figure out how to get in to see a buyer. I have often been able to bring the two together and the results are gratifying.

The last set of reasons for writing this book is the philosophical ones. I am excited about the changing role of American women. The heightened self-awareness and increasing sense of self-worth are dynamic and positive indicators that the historic oppression of females is lessening. Many of the women's liberation organizations have worked to change federal legislation, opening up broader life-style choices for all women. However, legislation and official recognition are only a small part of what is needed for a true metamorphosis. A personal change of attitude, a fresh point of view are necessary to complete the picture. The "Oh, I can't do anything" must truly give way to "I can do anything I want to."

I have heard many women talk about their unfulfilling lives in terms of economic dependency. Too often a woman stays in an unsatisfactory marriage because she feels unable to earn much of a living for herself—and perhaps for her children as well. Or she stays in a job she hates because she feels trapped in an impossible situation where no other work can be found or the thought of giving up a pension renders her immobile.

How to Make Money with Your Crafts is addressed particularly to women in this sense: for a woman to change her situation and feelings of dependency usually must be a process rather than an instant happening. A well-developed hand skill can be a tool to be used, helping the woman move into a more independent position, acquainting or re-acquainting her with the world of business.

Confidence builds as little successes plainly show, beyond a doubt, that Ms. I-Can't-Do-Anything has a lot more going for her than she once thought. True, a tiny business is not going to be the solution to all problems, but the knowledge that one can operate easily in the business world opens up a wealth of alternatives.

But, further, I feel that people in general—by no means women in particular—make too much of a division between their "jobs" and their "lives." Too often the job becomes drudgery, work necessary to earn a living, and the non-work time is the "rest" of life, all that is left for activity one enjoys.

I prefer the idea that one's total output of activity is one's "life." Some parts of the activity will be money-making, others will not. And as the person grows and expands, the activities which bring in money will change, phasing in and out as temperaments and situations change.

Economists have noted a trend toward the multi-skilled worker, equipped to earn money in several un-related fields. This trend is sometimes chalked up to tight money, recession, or diminishing job markets which make moonlighting a necessity. I doubt that necessity is the sole motivation behind this phenomenon. I am more inclined to believe that people are realizing that the things they enjoy doing are the things they do best and can get paid for if they choose.

So the last of my reasons for writing this book is to help hurry in the era of the multi-skilled person who can pick and choose many combinations of activities from which to earn a living. Economic independence, or the feeling that economic independence can become a reality, creates positive changes for a freer future. This reason has nothing to do with whether the readers of this book are men or women. For all craftspersons today there is a need their skills can fill—a need for authenticity and honest quality in the things that people use, wear, live with, look at, and love. This need can be filled with realistic, economic good sense and this book is for anybody who wants to set forth and learn how.

How to Use This Book

The amount of use this book will be to you depends, of course, on how committed you really are to starting a business, and on how you are planning to conduct that business. I have provided the following chapter breakdowns to help you readily find the information that will be the most useful and relevant to you.

—If you are shopping around for an appropriate way to market your crafts, the following chapters will help define some of the alternatives:

Chapter I: Estimating Your Business Potential
Chapter II: Making Your Business Legitimate
Chapter III: Where to Go for Professional Advice
Chapter IV: Defining *Your* Customer
Chapter X: Publicity and Promotion
Chapter XI: Craft Fairs and Outdoor Art Shows
Chapter XII: Art Galleries and Mail Order

—If you have decided to sell or are occasionally selling a few things to local people, but are not interested in becoming a tycoon, check:

Chapter I: Estimating Your Business Potential
Chapter II: Making Your Business Legitimate
Chapter III: Where to Go for Professional Advice
Chapter VI: Bookkeeping, Accounting and Other
    Financial Considerations
Chapter VII: Costing
Chapter XI: Craft Fairs and Outdoor Art Shows
Chapter XII: Art Galleries and Mail Order

—If you are planning or have already opened a small shop or boutique, look into:

Chapter II: Making Your Business Legitimate
Chapter III: Where to Go for Professional Advice
Chapter IV: Defining *Your* Customer (Home Furn-
    ishing and Fashion Magazines sections)
Chapter V: The "Trade": What It Is and
    How You Use It
Chapter VI: Bookkeeping, Accounting and
    Other Financial Considerations
Chapter VII: Costing
Chapter VIII: Purchasing and Manufacturing
Chapter X: Publicity and Promotion

—If you are planning or have started building a wholesale volume business, concentrate on:

Chapter II: Making Your Business Legitimate
Chapter III: Where to Go for Professional Advice
Chapter IV: Defining *Your* Customer
Chapter V: The "Trade": What It Is and
    How You Use It
Chapter VI: Bookkeeping, Accounting and
    Other Financial Considerations
Chapter VII: Costing
Chapter VIII: Purchasing and Manufacturing
Chapter IX: Seeing a Buyer
Chapter X: Publicity and Promotion

—If you are strictly a one-of-a-kind designer, more artist than entrepreneur, turn to:

Chapter II: Making Your Business Legitimate
Chapter VI: Bookkeeping, Accounting and
      Other Financial Considerations
Chapter X: Publicity and Promotion
Chapter XI: Craft Fairs and Outdoor Art Shows
Chapter XII: Art Galleries and Mail Order

And, above all—good luck!

chapter I

Estimating Your Business Potential

Since you are looking through this book I already know a little bit about you. You have a craft or skill that you enjoy doing. It might have been your hobby since childhood or it might be something that caught your fancy mere months ago. But you get a lot of pleasure out of it and you feel that the items you make are pretty good. Or very good. Or perhaps even superb.

You might have been introduced to your craft through a store-bought kit as in the case of knitting, crocheting, needlework, rugs or macramé. Numerous leatherworkers have told me they became interested through belt or bag kits. The paint-by-the-numbers sets have launched many a craftsperson into decorative fashion and home accessories.

Perhaps the free sewing instruction course offered when you bought your sewing machine was the beginning of your craft. Or the fashion publicity about tie-dyeing sent you off to the store to pick up one of the give-away pamphlets the dyestuff companies were offering.

However you got there, you are, at this moment, a craftsperson/designer. You may or may not have sold anything you've made. The initial products the beginner turns out are usually saved for his own use or given to loving friends and relatives. How many of us have purred with delight when the recipient of our wonderful gift has been really overwhelmed not only at the gift itself but at the fact that we, their erstwhile ten-thumbed buddy, just whipped it up ourself! There is a satisfaction to be had not only from practicing your craft well but from the response you get as each new finished product is unveiled.

So you continued to make things, venturing into more complex designs as your skills grew. For most of us the next step was when we contributed a few things to the church fair, the P.T.A. bazaar or some other community fund-raising event. As we stood near the counter and watched total strangers browse by, pick up our contributions and pay actual money to take them home and own them forever, a definite mental connection was made. Money had just been exchanged for something we had made. Our items were salable. Extra income was ours if we wanted it.

Once the initial mental connection is made a multitude of exciting alternatives are open to you. You may decide to try selling small quantities or individual items to friends and acquaintances, augmenting your income a bit while you continue in your current life style. Or you may fantasize building up a huge, successful business empire, complete with elegant offices, nationwide television advertising, and you on the cover of *Time* magazine as that creative genius who made a million overnight. Don't we all remember the hula hoop?

No matter which alternative you decide on, an amount of quiet introspection and diligent soul-searching is required before you take action. In fairness to yourself, your family and your friends, you must think through your plans with regard to who you are, where you are and what kind of life you are currently leading.

DO YOU HAVE THE TIME?

To begin with, going into business, no matter how small, is a lot of work. Are you willing to devote vast amounts of your concentration to it? Do you really want to sell your things enough to rearrange some of your life to make it happen? Are you willing to stick to it when the going gets rough?

How many hours in your week are available to put into your business? What other demands are made on your free time? If you are working full time your free hours are severely restricted, but your office might be in midtown so you could get out easily during lunch hours to do your market work. If you are raising young children, keeping house, caring for older relatives and are generally house-bound your free hours are also severely limited. You might find you can sandwich in handwork time during naps or quiet hours, but getting out to the marketplace will pose a problem.

An honest estimate of your available time is important. If you are counting evenings as potential work periods take into account your normal dinner hour. If you dine at six o'clock, a work period can logically begin at about seven-thirty. If dinner generally gets on the table at eight you probably won't get much work done until after nine-thirty. The simple matter of rescheduling dinner to an early hour might be the answer but would it work out for the rest of your household?

Consider your personal mobility. Going into business, whether you want to sell a few things or many, means you will have to spend a fair amount of time in the stores near you and in locating and dealing with local wholesalers for product supplies. Your accessibility to a Post Office that will take larger size packages figures in if you hope to sell to outlets outside of your own neighborhood. Once you have considered the distances you will have to travel often and easily you will be able to judge whether or not your mobility is sufficient for the amount of business you plan to do. Do you drive a car or is there public transportation readily available?

DO YOU HAVE THE SPACE?

Extra space within your home is a factor, no matter how modest your business plans are. In order to get a reduced price for your materials you will be expected to buy in larger quantities than you have been buying. The larger quantities will have to be stored someplace where they will be kept clean and easily available. Can you arrange for such space without crowding another person or will you eventually have to purchase a storage cabinet?

If your business plans are ambitious and you hope to build a company with sizable sales volume is there extra space available locally that you could eventually rent? Check your local newspapers and get a general idea of what commercial work space is renting for in your community. Space planning is important. Eventually even the most creative designer gets upset when the whole house is filled with cardboard cartons, half-finished items, and living seems to have turned into camping out.

DO YOU HAVE THE CAPITAL?

Think about money. Setting up any sort of small business requires a certain amount of capital. You will have extra transportation costs just to get out into the market. You will be buying amounts of raw materials. Even your telephone bill will increase. These things, and many more, will cause extra expenses during your first year. Frightening statistics from the United States Small Business Administration point out that over 60 percent of all new businesses fail within the first year of operation due to undercapitalization. Don't be part of next year's 60 percent.

It is difficult, in fact impossible, to estimate your projected expenses down to the last dollar. However, think about costs (see Chapter VI and Chapter VII), check whatever figures are available to you on wholesale prices, packaging, stationery, etc. You will come up with an educated guess as to your initial capital. It might range from a scant hundred dollars up to a couple of thousand. Bear in mind that the figure you arrive at will not be gospel truth. But it will give you a general idea into what area your money needs fall.

Then you can compare this figure with your bank balance, your extra cash, your piggy bank, your allowance or anyplace else you can think of as a logical money source. If you feel you will have to borrow money during your first year, do you know somebody you can borrow from? It is important that you do not get bogged down in depressing, time-consuming money planning, but it is also important that you get some over-all picture of what you will need.

A good antidote for the gloom that often settles in when you estimate expenses is to shift quickly over to consider what your extra-income needs are. Of course people who think about going into business want to make as much money as possible. But quite separate from the wishful-thinking sum is the amount of income you would consider necessary to make it all worthwhile. You pretty much know your yearly expenses. Is your need for extra income related to your yearly expenses? Is your need for extra income related to some outside cost such as sending children through school, buying a vacation home, paying off a debt or mortgage? Are your income needs seasonal or all year round? Would you like to have extra cash for smashing summer travel holidays, or are you more interested in a small lump sum each month to ease you through your everyday expenses?

Think about it. Do you actually need to make a lot of extra money in the coming twelve months? If so, starting your own business offers you less quick income potential than going out and working for other people or taking work home to do for a business. Getting any business launched is a long-range project full of triumphs and mistakes. Don't count on the money rolling in during the first year.

I must confess, some of my own initial reasons for wanting to make a bit of extra money were to buy a dishwasher and to hire a maid. Sounds rather petty, I admit, and I would like to be able to say I started my own business to make the world better for mankind, or to create beautiful things that would brighten people's lives, but the fact remains—I simply wanted to lighten my work load. And I had made the connection that items I was producing were salable.

Whatever your personal reasons are for wanting extra money, think them through until you have some clear picture of how much money you would like to make (within reason) and what timing you would prefer for getting that money. Once you arrive at an answer you have set a goal for yourself. You now know How Much Is Enough. You have something to aim at, a guideline that will help you decide whether or not you are accomplishing what you set out to do. There will be days when you'll wonder what you've gotten yourself into. Keep your goal in mind. It helps to realize you wanted to go from zero extra income to a certain amount of money per month, and you are partially there!

YOUR ATTITUDE TOWARD YOUR WORK

As you make the gradual transition from a hobbyist to a professional designer/manufacturer/craftsperson you will find that certain of your attitudes must be changed. The hobbyist views his finished products as extensions of himself, each one a "child" he has created. The professional designer, on the other hand, has a more impersonal attitude toward his creations. He is in business to make money, not to make pretty things to please himself. That is a difficult transition to make, depersonalizing your products to the point where you design and produce items you feel will sell, and you toss out items and designs that are not overly salable.

Begin to make that attitudinal change as soon as possible. It will be painful, but might well mean the difference between a successful business and a bankruptcy. If opening your own business is merely an ego-trip for you, then you will continue to view your products as your children. If you are serious about wanting to make money you must begin to separate your personal involvement from your business judgment.

SEPARATING SKILLS FROM PRODUCTS

A good way of beginning the transition is to divide your skill from your products. You skill is the sum total of all the information you have gathered about your craft, plus all the working knowledge you have acquired from the many hours you have spent working. For example, if you are a knitter your skill covers your knowledge of stitches, patterns, sizing, yarns and threads, needles, finishing, blocking, pressing, plus all the deft movements your hands know how to make while creating a knitted item. Your skill, then, is everything you possess that enables you to design and make up a product.

Your product, on the other hand, is the item you have produced with your skill. With your one skill you will produce many, many products. Some will be sold, some given away, some kept and cherished, some copied by every competitor you have in the market. View your products as almost disposable. You make them and they go away from you. Your skill will never go away from you and will increase with each item you design and produce.

I am often amused by new designers who are deathly afraid of being copied—"knocked off" as we say in the trade. They feel that their best designs will be stolen and they will be left with nothing. What they don't realize is that their skill can never be stolen, which is far more important than any one design.

True, it is infuriating to see some other company

making money from one of your designs. And it happens every day. On the other hand, a person who has never designed something that is worth copying is not much of a designer. In an odd way, the more your designs are copied the more you know you are on the right track, creating exactly what the market is looking for.

There is no way of protecting a design once it is for sale in a public place. Anyone who wants to copy you can buy one of your items, take it back to his factory, make some tiny, almost invisible change and come out with his own "interpretation" of the product. And if your design is good he will make lots of money on the product, especially if he can cut the price down a bit and give the buyer a break.

But you can console yourself with the firm knowledge that your skill created a winner and can and will create many, many more. And you can complain loudly to everyone in the trade about being copied. They will know what you mean!

EVALUATING YOUR PRODUCTS

Once you are clear on the separation between your skill and your products, it's time to give your products an impersonal inspection. Take a few items out, place them in front of you and examine them carefully. Consider how they would look if they were placed along with other items on display in a shop. Is the workmanship as good as similar products now on the market? Are the items finished neatly? Poor finishing is so often the mark of the novice. Are your color and texture choices commercially acceptable, i.e., looking kind of like the other merchandise on the shelf, or are they too off-beat to have mass appeal?

If you can't decide how your work compares to your

competitors', take a walk through a store or two that carries merchandise similar to yours. Look closely at how everything is designed and put together. Bear in mind that the buyer for the store has shopped around and has selected this merchandise as being the most salable, most attractive, and least likely to be returned to his store.

Decide what you believe to be the strong points of your items. What do you feel makes them a bit better than others you have seen in stores and in the magazines? Are they better made, more colorful, more practical, easier to wear or use, prettier or more delicate? What do you think would make the customer reach for your product rather than select the one sitting next to yours on the shelf?

Each consumer has only a limited amount of money to spend for the things he needs. Your products must compete for their share of the consumer's dollar. The consumer is going to buy somebody's items. How can you get him to spend his money on yours? Look your things over with that in mind. See how your products stack up in the competitive marketplace.

Then study the group again to determine what you can see as the weak points of your products. This will not be easy since you are still making the transition from hobbyist to professional. Chances are, either you will not be able to spot many weak points or you will stare until you decide they are all awful, and you will remain depressed all day. Neither reaction is accurate, of course. Even if a person has been a professional designer for years there will still be weak points that could stand improvement. Conversely, no item will be a complete and total failure.

Try to get a perspective on your products. Develop

a point of view about the strong points. You'll eventually want to mention the strong points to buyers when you show your line, so you might as well get to know them from the very beginning. Don't hesitate to announce that your unique use of color or interesting blending of materials makes this or that item very unusual and thus better than everything else that's around. You might practice statements like these behind closed doors until you achieve the correct amount of cool confidence necessary to make a believable delivery.

ASSESSING YOUR BUSINESS PERSONALITY

The last bit of introspection deals with whether or not you want to and are able to become a "boss." If you decide you want to build a business that does enough sales volume for you to hire workers, then you suddenly will find yourself The Boss. Some people can handle the situation marvelously and others find it intolerable. If you have chosen to build up a "big" small business, give it some thought. Are you able to give instructions clearly? Do you mind giving orders? Are you willing to supervise workers and to fire them if their work is not acceptable?

Are you willing to accept total responsibility for running the business? Are you dependable, and usually willing to stand by your word even if unpleasant situations follow? We've all been workers. Now try to visualize yourself as the boss. Does the role suit you? Are you willing to be The Big Rat if necessary?

Take your time going over all the points in these pages. They are important and will help you decide which of the many alternatives would be best for you in setting up your own business. If you find you have limited time, space, money, mobility, or any combination of these, tailor your goal with these in mind. Your chances of succeeding increase a thousandfold if your goal is a realistic one. Perhaps you will find you would be wiser to start out a bit more modestly than you had first supposed. Make your second goal the expansion of your tiny but solid business!

For a clearer view, take a pencil and fill in the following questionnaire. And above all—be honest!

1: How many hours in your week are available to put into your business _36 ou mdee_

2: What other demands are made on your time _Meals, laundry, cleaning, taxi, people_

3: Do you have unlimited personal mobility or are you home- or office-bound most of the daytime hours _have ear_

4: Do you have sufficient space in which to work _No !_

5: Can you make provision for expansion _?_

6: What will the extra space cost _?_

7: Do you have sufficient money—not slated for anything else—to begin your business _No_

8: Do you know where to get additional money _No_

9: Are your money needs $500 or less _Yes_
$1000 or less _____
$5000 or less _____

10: Do you need a lot of income per month or a little _So - So_

11: Do you need extra income year round or seasonally _year round_

12: What is your skill _Macamé, sewing, knitting, crochet, needlepoint, painting_

13: What are your products _____
_____

14: Number of sales made during the past 12 months
20 Santas, 1 clown, 3 day+soap, lots of soap

15: What is the price range of your products _____
_____

16: Are your products of professional quality _____
20¢ - $5.00

17: Is your skill up to professional standards *I think so.*
_____

18: List three strong points about your products
well made
good quoility Materials
fair prices

19: List three weak points about your products
No Package
Time to Make in consideration to price
_____

20: What steps can you take to improve the three
weak points _____
_____

21: Can you accept the responsibility of running
a business *yes*
_____

22: Have you had other experience being a boss
No

23: Can you tell other people what to do *I think so.*
_____

24: Do you stand by your word or can you be
swayed _____
_____

25: What is your professional goal five years from
today _____
_____

chapter II

Making Your Business Legitimate

Once you've decided to "go into business," "sell a few things," "try to make a little money" or whatever your phrase for it is, there are only three ways to go about it. You can decide to have one of the following:

A: Individual Proprietorship
B: Partnership
C: Corporation

That's all. Of course there are multitudes of variations on partnerships and corporations but the basic structure is still there. Each of the choices has distinct advantages and disadvantages.

INDIVIDUAL PROPRIETORSHIP

Individual proprietorship means *you* go into business—just you under your own name or under a trade name. You are legally responsible for everything, personally liable for everything you buy or contract, and you can be sued personally if anything goes wrong. Which means that everything you own personally can be wiped out if you were sued and lost the suit.

On the brighter side, setting yourself up as an individual business person requires no legal work, costs no money and takes no time. You just get up one day and say, "I'm in business." Also, if it's only you running the business, making the decisions, calling the shots, you alone decide which risks to take and thus have individual, personal control over liability situations that could get you in trouble.

PARTNERSHIP

Partnership means that you and one or more people go into business together under some or all of your names or under a trade name. There may or may not be anything equal in a partnership—equal investment of time, work or money, and equal say in the short- and long-range plans—and decisions about the business. It all depends on how you and the other people set it up.

But one thing is very, very equal in a partnership. That is the fact that each person involved is personally liable for all the purchases, debts and contracts of the entire business.

In other words, when you enter into a partnership you tell the world that you will be fully responsible for everything your partners do, businesswise, not just your share of the debts, contracts, etc. You might be one of a group of four partners and end up having to pay off all the bad debts yourself if something terrible happens.

Of course you, in turn, could then sue the other partners for the monies you had paid. But it would be messy. Partnerships, when they work out, are wonderful. But they are as tricky as marriages. Just look at the divorce rate.

CORPORATION

The third choice, the corporation, offers you the most personal protection, but it must be set up by a lawyer, it costs money and it takes a bit of time. A corporation could be described as an artificial person created by law. The corporation/person is separate and distinct from the stockholders and the officers of the corporation. The corporation/person is totally liable for all debts and contracts of the business. If things go wrong and the business fails, the assets of the corporation are all that can be claimed in order to pay off creditors. The real people running the corporation cannot be held liable, and their own personal property is safe from any claims.

An interesting note on corporations is that often people inadvertently assume personal liability innocently. It's quite simple. All business done by the corporation must be conducted in the name of the corporation. If anyone else's name is used then that person is responsible. For example, if a messenger delivers some material to a corporation's workroom, the person who receives the shipment will be asked to sign a receipt. That receipt must be signed "XYZ Corporation—Jane Smith" in order to keep the corporation liable. If the receiver goofs and just signs "Jane Smith" the responsibility and thus the liability for that shipment is automatically assumed by Jane Smith. The corporation has never entered into the transaction!

Those are your three choices for setting up your own business. Albeit the most risky, small businesses usually start out as individual proprietorships. Then they might progress through a partnership stage, or just grow right into a corporation. In any case, whichever one you choose, it's wise to understand your liabilities.

LICENSES AND PERMITS

Having made your decision, the next step is letting the necessary authorities know you are open for business. The "authorities" in most cases turn out to be the State Departments of Taxation or Revenue. Basically your state wants to know who you are, where you are, and what type of business you are conducting. In most states, it is against the law to operate a business without a permit or license. Be *sure* you check!

Some of the larger cities and towns also have local permits, licenses or tax arrangements, but the state is really the major factor. The requirements in almost all fifty states are remarkably similar. Square yourself away with the state people and then be sure to inquire about local rules for operating a business.

Mailing addresses for all State Departments of Taxation or Revenue are listed in Appendix I, page 199. Write a brief note to the Department in your state telling them that you are opening a small business and would like them to send you information about all regulations pertinent to your situation, and any application forms for necessary licenses or permits. Be very specific about your business, including:

1. The complete name and address, specifying if it is the same or different from your personal name and address

2. Whether it is an individual proprietorship, a partnership or a corporation
3. Type of business, i.e., wholesale, retail or a combination of both
4. A general description of your products including a mention of which raw materials you are using, e.g., leather, fur, etc.
5. Also ask if there is a local office you could be dealing with rather than writing to the state capital.

The state will send you all sorts of literature, instructions and application forms for any necessary permits or licenses. Occasionally there is a small fee charged for the registering of a business, but most often it is a free service. The forms, without exception, are simple and much easier to fill out than the federal income tax forms. It is a good idea to keep all the data together so you can refer to it if questions come up as your business grows.

Getting necessary licenses is a step too often skipped by beginners. Maintaining a low profile is sometimes held to be an advantage, illegal though it may be. However, if you are going to operate within the business community you need the recognition and also the proof that you are not just a hobbyist but are actually making and selling your designs. In addition, it is the only way you can legitimately buy your supplies wholesale. Be smart and don't put off writing that letter!

SALES TAX

As to the tax data—the big concern is with the retail sales tax, which is added on to the selling price of items destined for direct sale to the consumer. The amount of sales tax varies widely in different states from absolutely nothing to quite a bit, and also varies in different areas within each state due to extra local tax levies. But it is always tacked on over the selling price, and is the money the retailer passes back to the State Bureau of Taxation. Since the sales tax money is generally a sizable part of a state's revenue, they want to keep track of all retail businesses in their territory.

So if you are planning to sell your items direct to the consumer you will have to add the sales tax on top of your own selling price, and periodically pass the tax money you collect back to the state government. When you apply for your permit or license to do business you will be asked to indicate on the application form whether you are selling retail or wholesale. If you are retailing you will receive instructions on how much tax you should collect per dollar value of your products and the manner in which you must file your records and send back the tax money.

Things are different if you are wholesaling your items to retailers who will place your things in their stores and do the actual selling to the consumer. In that case you are not retailing and do not have to collect any sales tax. Again, you will indicate this on the permit application form.

TAX EXEMPTION OR RESALE CERTIFICATES

For both retailing and wholesaling you will receive information on how to issue "tax exemption certificates" to the people you are buying your raw materials from. The exemption certificates will prove that you are recognized by your state as either a wholesaler who is purchasing goods to make up products which will be sold to a store, or as a retailer who is purchasing goods to be made up into products to be sold direct to a consumer.

You are not expected to pay any retail sales tax on the materials you buy for use in products you plan to resell. Which is a small blessing. The real benefit you get from being recognized, i.e., licensed by your state to be a retailer or a wholesaler, and the big argument in favor of letting the authorities know what you are doing, is that your permit number establishes without a doubt that you are legitimately in business and thus entitled to buy materials at wholesale prices. Now THAT's a benefit—without which your costing figures are way off!

Most states have a general form they send you to follow for your exemption certificates. A typical certificate might be typed on your business stationery, or just on plain paper, and would read something along these lines:

"I hereby certify that this purchase is for resale in the regular course of business, or is to be used as an ingredient or component part of a new article of tangible personal property to be produced for sale."

Registration No. _____

Name as Registered _____

Firm Name _____

Address _____

Type of Business _____

Authorized Signature _____ Title _____

Date _____

You will either give or send an exemption certificate

to any company you buy supplies from to make up your products. You cannot issue exemption certificates, and/ or claim tax exemptions on purchases of tools or machinery with which you make up your items—only materials that pass through your hands and then go on to the consumer may be tax-exempt.

Most states allow you to issue one blanket exemption certificate to each company you make multiple purchases from so you don't have to do the paper work each time you go shopping. Your suppliers, when they file their tax records with the authorities, will list your company as having bought materials from them for the purpose of reselling, to show why they do not have sales tax money to give back on the amount of supplies you bought.

chapter III

Where to Go for Professional Advice

U. S. SMALL BUSINESS ADMINISTRATION

If you are looking for free advice it's hard to beat the United States Small Business Administration. A branch of the Government, funded out of our tax dollars, the S.B.A. was set up in 1953 under the wing of the Eisenhower Administration. The proposal to Congress to create the S.B.A. described its function as ". . . to support and promote small business and to be totally responsive to the needs of the small-business community," which it seems to be doing admirably.

S.B.A. is headed up by an over-all administrator located in Washington, D.C. Employing around four thousand people, it is the smallest of all the federal agencies. To facilitate its operation S.B.A. has divided the United States into ten regions with seventy-seven regional offices, plus branches. It works out that wherever you are there is an S.B.A. office nearby. Locations are listed in Appendix II on page 204.

The S.B.A. definition of a small business ranges from a one-person operation to a 1,500-person operation, depending on the industry. Thus the size of a business is judged against what else is in that specific field. S.B.A. considers that 94 percent of all manufacturers and wholesalers are small businesses. Of course some are a lot smaller than others.

S.B.A. Publications

There are many services the S.B.A. offers that might be of value to you. First are its publications, both free and for sale, covering topics of interest to a small-business owner. Lists of these booklets are available at any S.B.A. office. Typical booklets are:

Checklist for Going into Business
Apparel & Accessories for Women, Misses and
    Children
Handicrafts and Home Business
Analyze Your Records to Reduce Costs
Are You Kidding Yourself About Your Profits?
The ABC's of Borrowing
Knowing Your Image
Steps in Meeting Your Tax Obligation

And many, many more. Among the for-sale booklets, none costs over $1.25 per copy with many in the 30¢-to-50¢ range. Most of the material is written by experts from private industry who have something to say that's worth listening to.

S.B.A. Counseling Services

Other activities of S.B.A. are the management counseling services, S.C.O.R.E., Service Corps of Retired Executives, and A.C.E., Active Corps of Executives. The agency estimates that nine out of ten business failures are due to managerial deficiencies that could have been avoided if the deficient management had had the proper advice at the proper time. To remedy this, the first line of consultants is the S.C.O.R.E. staff—groups of retired business executives who have volunteered their time to form a pool of knowledgeable people available to small businesses.

Retailers, production analysts, foreign trade specialists, office managers, scientists, lawyers, management consultants, engineers, wholesalers, accountants, advertising and public relations people, economists and bankers are some of the many experts who comprise the S.C.O.R.E. roster. To tap into this wellspring of information all you have to do is contact your local S.B.A. office and ask them to put you in touch with a S.C.O.R.E. staffer who can talk to you about whatever area of your business is puzzling you.

In all fairness, you should have your needs rather well thought out and your questions concisely framed so the S.C.O.R.E. person can be as helpful as possible. It is not his job to ferret out the difficulty—it is yours, but then he can help you solve it.

The A.C.E. group of volunteers is similar to the S.C.O.R.E. group, but consists of active executives from major industries, the professions, trade associations and schools and colleges. These people take time out of their own work schedules to be available as consultants to small-business owners. The A.C.E. staff was created to augment the S.C.O.R.E. operation and to keep the counseling on a current, updated basis.

Again, to be put in contact with an A.C.E. volunteer

you merely put in a request to your local S.B.A. office. Both groups are available to you at no cost whatsoever. In the event you want an A.C.E. or S.C.O.R.E. volunteer to come out and visit your studio in order to observe your production or other procedures, the volunteer's expenses are covered by the S.B.A. also.

In addition to the one-to-one consultations, S.B.A. runs periodic free management training courses, workshops and problem-solving clinics in or near every S.B.A. office. Many of these are all-day affairs, held on Saturdays, or evening sessions run by S.B.A. staff members. If you are interested in information on any of these, check your local S.B.A. office.

S.B.A. Business Loan Programs

The major role of S.B.A. is to deal with the financing of small businesses. The United States Government estimates that small businesses need sixteen billion dollars in credit each year. The S.B.A. is set up to help that happen, in several money-securing programs.

The first program is a loan guarantee arrangement in which the S.B.A. cooperates with local bankers to help a business borrow money. The way it actually works is this: the business owner goes to the local bank and requests a small-business loan, from amounts as small as five hundred dollars up to many times that amount. The banker reviews the loan application and ends up feeling that the bank cannot grant the loan as requested for one reason or another. That's where the S.B.A. comes in—after the loan application has been rejected by the bankers.

The business owners may then discuss with the banker the option of asking the S.B.A. to review the loan application. The application is handed over to the loan officers at a local S.B.A. office who decide whether or not the S.B.A. will guarantee to back up the majority of the loan from the bank. In this way many small-business people who would not otherwise be able to raise capital find they can become eligible for bank loans. The bank, of course, is relieved of much of the risk of lending to new or perhaps relatively unestablished business people. It's like having the United States Government act as your cosigner.

The above explanation is a vast simplification of the actual process. Still, the result is to arrange credit for persons who might otherwise be turned down at a bank. It's worth thinking about!

Another financing program at S.B.A. is a much more limited one in which direct loans are made to selected small businesses which cannot find any bank that will lend them money. This gets pretty individual so I will not go into more detail here. However, amounts of money are loaned direct and it's a good thing to know about, at least as a last resort.

Some other S.B.A. programs might at some time be of interest to you. One is a plan available to minority-group members in which money is made available to ghetto residents and other disadvantaged persons to finance small businesses. Another is an emergency plan in which S.B.A. staffers go into disaster areas such as flood- or hurricane-damaged locales and work with the small businesses to reestablish their operations and channel emergency loan money in. Information on all the S.B.A. programs is available to you through the local S.B.A. offices.

Another source of free advice in certain parts of the country is the local counseling service, generally patterned after the S.B.A., and available through town chambers of commerce. New York City has an active Executive Volunteer Corps of retired business executives at 415 Madison Avenue, who are available from 10 A.M. to 3 P.M. each work day to give advice and counsel to small-business people. The Corps does not charge for the service, and handled over 6,000 cases last year, plus 100,000 telephone inquiries. The Executive Volunteer Corps, however, does not have any lending programs and does not guarantee bank loans.

BANKS

It would be a gross omission to write a chapter on professional advice without including your local bank as a fine place to get a bit of counsel. Of course the main business of any bank is its dealing with money, which I cover in another chapter, but banks are great for advice too.

As soon as your business plans are firmed up you will find you need a checking account separate from any other accounts you and your family might have. It's been proven time and time again that you court disaster whenever you try to mix business and personal monies in one bank account. Also, the local bankers are interested in you as part of the business community. By understanding your business and your plans the bank can better assist you in financial matters.

So head for your bank the first time you get some money in payment for products you have created and sold, and ask one of the bank officers to open a separate or business checking account. Usually you can count on getting a pretty nice reception from the banker, who will be interested in hearing about your products and your plans. Establishing a good, easy relationship with your banker is important. He will be looking for a direct, honest approach to who you are and where you are going. You may find that the first bank officer you deal with is simply not your cup of tea. Remember that a bank is made up of a number of personalities and you should look for one with whom you feel comfortable, somebody you would not hesitate to telephone or stop by and talk to if you had a question.

Once you have achieved rapport with your banker you can seek advice on business problems that are bothering you. Bankers, since they deal with businesses all day, are in a good position to know the ins and outs of the financial parts of companies. If you are considering making any major move or change you may want to check out your thinking with your banker and get some feedback on the pros and cons of your plans.

Bank Credit Information

Banks are great sources for credit information. If you get a sizable order from a small store or customer who is not familiar to you, you can call your banker and ask if you can be given any credit information on the new account. It might just save you from an ugly situation, a loss of your time, effort and money. If a new customer does not turn out to have a good reputation you can gracefully ease out of the situation by saying you require cash before delivery on initial orders from new buyers.

If you find you are asking for a goodly number of credit checks your bank may eventually place a nominal charge on it as a business service they are rendering you.

However, I have found the banks I've dealt with were happy to help out—especially where the unknown-to-me customer had an account with the same bank. Banks won't tell you how much money anybody else has but they will tell you whether or not people are reliable, handle their money properly and conduct their banking business in a dependable fashion.

Conversely, of course, your suppliers can be going to their bankers or membership credit bureaus such as Dun and Bradstreet and asking for credit information on you. Dun and Bradstreet is the best known of the credit reporting and collection agencies, most of which operate quite similarly. If you need access to more credit information than your bank cares to supply, you can take out a membership in a credit reporting agency. Some sort of identification will be assigned to you and when you need to clarify somebody's credit you merely phone or write the agency, give your membership identification and are furnished with the data.

Costs vary widely since some agencies charge by the time period while others charge in relationship to the activeness of the account. If you find you need to join an agency, shop around to find one that best suits your specific situation. Sales representatives often assume the responsibility of checking credit—more about that in Chapter IX.

Which brings us back again to why your relationship with your banker is so important. You will be judged, more or less, in the business world by your track record. Banks have to be honest with your record as well as everyone else's.

If your bank record shows you have a propensity toward overdrafts, mis-dating or other foibles the bank will have to look on those as unsatisfactory and relate their experience to the inquirer. Unfortunately that's the kind of statement that may dog your tracks for a long while.

Ms. Marion F. Schappel, Vice President of the First National City Bank of New York, puts it simply: "Don't play games with your checkbook." Find out from your banker exactly how many days it takes for local and out-of-town checks to clear through so you can know when you have the actual use of the money in your account. Just handing a bank teller checks along with a deposit slip is not enough. *You are responsible for the checks if they are returned unpaid and you have already used the money.*

Banks will give you knowledgeable investment advice if and when you reach the stage of wanting to take some money out of your business. Ask and they will tell you what sort of interest-bearing investments they know about that would be pertinent to you. The even larger company can ask the bank to act as trustee or investor for pension and profit-sharing plans. There really is a lot more to a bank than deposits and withdrawals!

ACCOUNTANTS

Another person who will be able to give you advice —not for free, however—is an accountant. He or she can look at your finances objectively, tell you if you are headed in the right direction, and perhaps suggest changes that might make your money dealings more efficient. Accountants are past masters at simplifying the maze and muddle of government regulations and local, state and federal tax requirements. They can present you with a brief synopsis of what all the authorities expect from you and even draw up a timetable so you can see what your part of the process must be each month.

Whether or not you need to consult an accountant is totally personal. If you feel uneasy about your understanding of your money matters, it is a good idea to check it all out with a professional. Often the peace of mind justifies the extra expense!

Very small businesses do not require the services of an accountant on a regular basis. You can easily handle the billing and the bookkeeping yourself. However, once you get big enough to hire workers you should make life easier for yourself by checking your systems out with a Certified Public Accountant. A consultation with a C.P.A. is not prohibitively expensive and most certainly will save you hours of wonder and worry as you get into dealing with Workman's Compensation forms and other employer headaches.

Locating an accountant is simple. Personal recommendations are best, so ask the business people you know for information about the accountants they work with. Your banker might be able to supply you with a name or two. However, shop around until you find an accountant you feel comfortable with.

Remember that he or she will need to know every intimate detail of your operation so keep looking until you come across someone you can trust and whose business judgment you have some respect for.

Many people use their very-small-business period to check on several accountants prior to needing an accountant's service full time. Accountants' fees vary but are usually on a time basis for initial consulting. When you call to make the first appointment be sure to ask about the consultation fee so you will fully understand what amount you will be paying for what amount of time.

LAWYERS

If and when your business gets large enough to employ several people you might require the services of an attorney, so it is a good idea to be on the lookout for a *simpatico* person you could work closely with. A lawyer can advise you in three areas:

1. By preparing proper contracts and agreements between you and others such as workers, landlords, equipment-leasing companies, truckers, etc.
2. By acquainting you with your legal position on government regulations such as zoning, pollution, union or contractor dealings, etc.
3. By handling any and all claims, threats or lawsuits that come your way.

Friends in business, your banker or your accountant are logical people to ask when you are looking for lawyers to consult. A nominal fee is standard for the first visit so be sure to inquire about the amount and the time you will be allotted.

Some lawyers are also accountants, which works out wonderfully. My own lawyer, Milton E. Maybruck of New York City, is both an attorney and C.P.A. and the combination has been advantageous time and again! Other lawyers and accountants have close working arrangements since their bailiwicks are often overlapping. If you find somebody you like, be sure to ask about this.

INSURANCE AGENTS

Another individual advice-giver is an insurance agent. His or her advice is generally free and will tell you what types of insurance coverage might be helpful for a business of your size. As your business grows, you will accumulate pieces of equipment—for example, looms, sewing and cutting machines, wood-working tools, etc., and also quantities of raw materials. When you own substantial amounts of things, it is smart to look into fire and theft insurance just as it is with valuable personal possessions. If you are working out of your home it is a good idea to consult with the insurance agent who handles your home policy. Often a few minor changes can extend an on-going policy to cover your raw materials and equipment.

I have never found it necessary to select an insurance agent with the extreme care needed for a banker, an accountant and a lawyer. My financial soul is bared for the latter three. My insurance agent is a much more distant helper, necessary, but less intimate.

The main thing all these professionals have in common is that they offer time-saving simplifications to the small-business owner. Most of us could, if necessary, wade through the rules and regulations and come out with some sort of comprehension. Still, your time is valuable and it's economically more sound to get fast, easily understandable advice that you can put to work for you the minute you get it.

A final note of advice—as soon as word gets around that you are a designer you will find that everyone you come in contact with suddenly has become an expert critic. From the delivery boy and the cleaning woman to your family and friends, everyone will be happy to tell you what to do. One memorable day I had a garment up on my dress form and I was re-draping a sleeve. The postman poked his head in to give me the mail, studied the garment a moment or two and suggested I put a few bows on it to make it prettier. I thanked him kindly and kept the door locked after that. Still, to quote an old family adage, "The best thing about advice is that you don't have to take it."

chapter IV

Defining Your Customer

Now that you have gotten the size, shape and goal of your business venture established it is time to figure out exactly who your potential customer is. In order to sell your products you have to find a buyer. If you've decided to sell direct to the consumers, that is, selling on the retail level, your customer-hunt is a relatively easy one. The men and women you live near, work with and socialize with are all potential buyers. Your products can be almost custom made, tailored to the buyer's personal taste.

But if you've decided to go the wholesale route and sell small quantities of the products to buyers in retail stores, it's all a different story. Buyers lurk in certain parts of your town, are sometimes known to be elusive and evasive and often are difficult for the inexperienced buyer-hunter to locate. However, their natural habitat will be filled with products having the same general appeal as your products have. Once you locate a few

47

retail stores that are selling items that are similar in feeling and price range to yours, your buyer-hunt is nearing a successful completion.

TYPICAL CUSTOMER PROFILE

Retail stores, from tiny boutique shops to massive department stores, are designed to appeal to a specific customer. Retailers, smart folk that they are, know that they will be more successful aiming for one segment of the population, catering to the needs and tastes of that certain group rather than trying to sell everything to everybody.

Successful retailers can describe their typical customer in great detail. They can tell you the customer's age bracket, income level, educational background, family structure, marital status, social life, reading habits, living conditions and many other intimate details! These retailers have singled out one category of consumers and have created a store that will appeal to them. From the merchandise to the window displays, to the shopping bags and even the bill enclosures, the taste of their typical customer is catered to. Nothing is left to chance.

To facilitate your buyer-hunt it is wise for you to think about an ideal or typical customer who would be interested in owning one of your creations. Are you designing for young people or older people? Are they traditional and elegant or are they into the latest fad as soon as it becomes recognized? Build up your own picture of the person you feel would be most likely to buy your products. There is no one product that has universal appeal. Your mother and your daughter will not be equally enchanted by the same item.

Think about your typical customer. He or she may be a duplicate of you, or a complete opposite. Regardless, it is important that you get to know *your* customer very well. The more data you have on likes and dislikes the better chance you have of becoming *your* customer's favorite designer. Each of us has our favorites —how many times have you returned from a shopping trip saying, "I really like so-and-so's clothes. They fit as though they were made for me!"

KNOW YOUR *CUSTOMER'S FAVORITE SHOPS*

Once you have visualized your typical customer it is time to make a walking tour of your local stores to see which ones are set up to appeal to the same category of customer that you are designing for. Get some idea of the price ranges the various stores and departments have. Check out the window displays and read the advertising.

Spend time in any department or corner of any store that has products that would be competitive to yours. Imagine your items next to the competitors' on the shelf. Notice what color groups seem to be in stock. Pick up any new ideas that you might want to add to your designs. Read a few labels if fiber content and fabric finishes are important to your products. Are the competitive products pre-packaged or presented in any unusual way? Check for the ratio of imported items versus American-made things. Some stores or departments are virtually "imports only" so to concentrate on them would be a waste of time.

READ YOUR *CUSTOMER'S FAVORITE MAGAZINES*

Your next research project is to become familiar with the magazines *your* typical customer is reading. Which, not so oddly, just happen to be the same magazines your potential retail-store buyer is reading. In every issue the editorial pages of these magazines are telling your customer what to wear or how to decorate her home. It is important that you tune in on the message also. You may determine that your typical customer is faithful reader of *Glamour* and *Mademoiselle*. Fine. Then you must become an equally faithful reader. If *House and Garden* and *House Beautiful* seem to cater to your typical customer, begin reading them yourself.

Make your next stop the reference room of your public library. Get out some back issues and current issues of the magazines your customer is reading. True, the consumer magazines will not tell you, a designer-manufacturer, what is happening on the wholesale level of your trade. There are separate trade magazines and newspapers that cover the latest news about designs, designers and manufacturers. Just make sure you know what your customer is being told first.

Products that are currently featured in the consumer magazines will be found on the shelves of your local stores during the month of publication. Generally the retailer has placed orders on this merchandise many months ahead. But since you are small enough to work on a tight time schedule and since you are a local supplier it is feasible for you to contact the retailer with items you can make up and deliver relatively fast. It is one of the advantages you have as a beginning business person, so don't pass it up!

The way you read a magazine for your business is a lot different from the way you read it for pleasure. In business you need to read to gather many kinds of information.

Often the first one-third on the magazine will be advertising pages with small columns of copy scattered among the ads. Fascinating as they are, the advertising pages are of no importance in your business reading. Eventually if you begin advertising in these magazines you will want to read the ads to keep tabs on your competitors. In the beginning skip the advertising pages.

Bernard Waldman, owner of Modern Merchandising Bureau, a New York advertising agency, puts it succinctly.

"My dear Ms. Clark," he would tell me, "you can buy a full page in *Vogue* or *Harper's Bazaar* and run a picture of the two of us if you want to. Or you can run a picture of your children and your dogs . . ."

His point is well taken. Magazines will accept almost anything that is not offensive or in questionable taste for their advertising pages. Paid advertising may or may not relate to the design, styling and fashion trends in any field. Generally a manufacturer will run an ad on an item he believes will become a best seller.

However, ads are also commonly used to "pay back" designers, fabric houses, fiber companies, or as part of cooperative retail store promotions, or even to dump merchandise that was unwittingly stocked. Advertising is in itself a very complex business. Suffice it to say here that the less you, the beginning business person, deduce from magazine advertising, the better.

In your library research skip over the pages until you get to the editorial section. This is the real meat of the magazine, where the editorial point of view is expressed. It is here that the retailer checks out his information, and it is here that your typical customer is sold on new looks, styles, colors and designs. It is here, too, that designers' names are mentioned, crediting them with the looks and styles that the magazine editors feel are important.

Editorial pages usually begin with a statement of the

theme of that issue of the magazine. "The Home of the Future" or "Rooms that Change with the Seasons" might be themes. Then the articles that follow the introductory page will illustrate and develop that theme with written copy, photographs and drawings.

HOME FURNISHING MAGAZINES

For example, say you are planning to sell pillows. You have determined that your typical customer is a faithful reader of *House Beautiful* and *House and Garden*. And if your typical customer is reading them, obviously the retail store buyer you are hoping to sell your pillows to is also reading them. It is imperative that you find out what these magazines are saying to both of them about room decor in general and pillows in particular.

There are certain points about pillows that you need to know. Are the pillows featured editorially large or small, square or round, rectangular or free-form shapes? Are they grouped on chairs and sofas or are they placed on the floor, singly or in stacks? Are the pillow covers solid colors, or are they patterned? Do they have fringes, tassels, braids, or other decorations, or are they relatively undecorated? Are the fabrics smooth or roughly textured? Make note of how many pillows featured in the editorial pages fall into what categories. Notice the colors. Are they muted or bright, light or dark?

While you are checking back and current issues of the magazines keep a running tally on the facts that interest you. After your reading time you can count up the numbers on your tallies and draw some conclusions that will aid you in designing and doing buyer contact work.

After tallying your data on pillows you might end up with information such as the following:

December issues of *House & Garden* and *House Beautiful*

A: Out of 105 editorial photos that could possibly use pillows, 97 of them showed pillows.

B: Of these 97 photos with pillows, 85 were very ornate, busy, patterned pillows. Lots of patch-work or pieced-together patterns.

C: Over 85 showed large pillows in square or geo-metric shapes. Sometimes the shape dictated or was echoed in the pieced-together, appliquéd or patchwork cover.

D: Very few pillows shown had any braid on them. None had tassels, fringes, etc.

E: Fabric covers were smooth-textured. No furs, loopy shags or leathers.

F: Pillows were grouped on floors and on furni-ture. They were used mainly in color-related groups, never alone. Seemed to be important parts of the room decor rather than additional accessories.

G: Colors were predominantly muted but clear; neither brilliant primary colors nor muddy, funky colors.

H: Ethnic patterns, i.e., Navajo blankets and In-dian paisleys, were used a lot.

These and any other facts you may feel are important will help you make your design decisions. The interpre-tation of the tallies is just common sense. You have just found that some of the major magazines are telling and showing your customer that big, interesting, important pillows with patterned (perhaps patchwork) covers will look great on her floor and her furniture. In clear but muted colors, sans tassels, fringes and other decorations.

So you start to think along those lines, if you haven't already, and make up your own interpretation of this look that you know is currently "in." If your personal design sense rebels at being restricted to the "in" look be sure to make up several other pillows that illustrate your own point of view. And then show both types to the retail store buyer when the time comes. The buyer will make the decision for you as to which is most salable in his shop.

Meanwhile you have a better chance at making a sale since you are showing pillows that follow the current trend. And you have included a few more radical designs of your own, different from the big, busy pillows seen in the market. Might be the next big seller for the adventurous pillow-buyer, something he'll take a chance on today, knowing trends come and go.

When you do show your line, take advantage of your library research time. Let the buyer know you are up on what is being promoted in magazines and newspapers. Discuss the "in" look if you have time. Ask about trends—is the big and busy pillow look going to be around much longer? Does the buyer see directions other than the ones you have shown as the next step in pillow design? Chances are any information you pick up will be useful. And it's another step in becoming knowledgeable about your field. A professional, not a hobbyist.

FASHION MAGAZINES

Reading the fashion magazines is done the same way as reading the home furnishing magazines. First you must narrow down exactly which publications your ideal customer will be reading. Perhaps she is a devotee of *Glamour* and *Mademoiselle*. Go to the library and get out back and current issues of both magazines. And begin to make your tally sheets for whatever your product category is.

Say, for example, you are making leather belts. Skip the advertising pages and begin checking every editorial photograph that could possibly show a belt. Are the belts shown wide or narrow? Patterned or plain, smooth-textured or grainy? Notice the size, shape and type of belt buckles and clasps that are used. Are there any sashes or long belt-ties featured?

After your reading time you might end up with a tally sheet such as this:

March Issues of *Glamour* and *Mademoiselle*

A: Out of 99 photographs that could possibly use belts, 70 showed belts of some kind.

B: Of the 70 belts shown, 57 were narrow leather belts. The other 13 were narrow belts made of the same fabric used in the garment.

C: No sashes or ribbon tie-belts were shown.

D: No belt seemed to be over 2 inches wide.

E: All leathers were smooth except for a few tooled leather cowboy belts on jeans outfits.

F: Buckles were very important, almost jewelry-like, adding to the total look rather than just fastening the belt ends together. Most buckles and clasps and other hardware were bright and shiny. No buckles were made totally of matte-finished metal although matte finishes were sometimes incorporated into the basic design of the belt buckle.

G: Belts were not used to cinch in waists. They were worn pretty much at the natural waistline, and were not drooping down at the buckle. Only the cowboy belts were worn low on the hips.

Interpreted, this tally will let you know that narrow belts with interesting, decorative buckles are important in today's fashion look for junior women. Most leathers shown are smooth and without apparent grain. Belts seem to be as much a part of the total costume as earrings, scarves, bags, etc. Sashes, ribbon-ties and other long flowing styles are simply not on the scene at the moment. Belts fit at the natural waist and give a rather trim look to the outfit.

So within the boundaries of narrow-up-to-2-inch widths, with smashing, decorative buckles, design two or three of the most marvelous belts you can dream up. But don't forget to include several others of your own preference. If you have a strong hunch that wide belts or sashes will be next in fashion, make up a few and show how you interpret these concepts. Your own numbers might prove to be the best sellers of the lot, but you are smart to show a few belts that relate to the current market. To a buyer your interpretation of the current fashion is every bit as important as your latest forecast-of-the-future belt.

All this magazine checking and store shopping might strike you as depressingly mechanical, and in a sense it does wipe out the "creative genius" designer fantasy. Contrary to myths and legends, no one designs in a vacuum. The stock-in-trade of the professional designer doing commercial work is her knowledge of her market, the trends, the promotional possibilities of the season. And, as one of my draping instructors used to remind our class of budding designers, "There are only so many ways to set in a sleeve." It's not art. It's business.

A fitting close to this chapter is a wonderful statement a too-well-known-to-be-identified designer friend once made to me. We had spent a grueling day in the market and he was at his most cynical. The talk came around, as it always does, to trends—what is new. He sighed and said wearily, "Honey, if the big color is red, you make it red. After that you are on your own . . ."

chapter V

The "Trade": What It Is and How You Use It

Strictly a slang expression whose origins are believed to go back to the medieval European craft guilds, "the trade" encompasses everyone connected with the creating, producing, selling or promoting of consumer goods. Making up "the trade" are all the professionals in your field, be they designers, editors, manufacturers, or the suppliers from whom you buy your raw materials.

An easy distinction between trade and non-trade is that the person who walks into a shop and buys a shirt to take home and wear is a consumer, i.e., not in the trade. The salesperson standing behind the counter is in the trade, backed up by all the people who have had a hand in the designing, manufacturing and promoting of that shirt up to the point that the consumer purchases it. The consumer is the end of the line for all trade activities. And all trade activities are in some way connected to luring the consumer into buying products, and buying them often!

Early in your business venture you will run across phrases such as "to the trade," "in the trade," "trade magazines," "trade papers." The use of the word "trade" defines the subject as being not of interest to the consumer. Conversely, trade means that the activity or subject is in some way related to and important to you, the new designer.

TRADE TREND INFORMATION

You, the small designer/manufacturer, need the trade for a variety of reasons. As we outlined in the last chapter, you can pick up data that will be helpful to you in designing your items if you sift through the consumer magazines' editorial sections on a regular basis. Additional trend information and important trend forecasts are available to you from other areas of the trade. For example, many of the major fiber producers and the American natural fiber councils publish and produce data forecasting the colors, lines, silhouettes and textures that their fashion and marketing experts feel will be the important looks for the coming seasons. These forecasts cover womenswear, menswear and home furnishings products and are used on a regular basis by the professional designers.

The fiber company or council basically puts out trend data in an attempt to increase the use of its product; handing out copies of its forecasts to customers on all levels of the trade, showing how its fiber will star in new applications.

The huge fabric producers are the first group of customers a fiber manufacturer wants to reach since they place the direct orders for fiber poundage, but the end product designers and the press are also pertinent. If the basic fiber producer can convince enough designers to begin asking for a certain color or a certain type of fabric (soft and drapey, stretchy, crisp, etc.) the mills are going to listen and order more fiber to fill the demand. It sounds a bit circuitous in the above simplification, but it's all part of creating a demand for a product on all levels in order to maintain an active equation between supply and demand.

Of course you are not a big customer of anything at all at the moment, but since these valuable forecasts are being done up anyway you might just want to tune in to them. Bear in mind that anything anybody produces is costly, and it's always seemed to me to be a bit unfair to ask for data you don't really need, but if the need is genuine, then definitely ask.

Since the big boys work far in advance you must plan to reach out for the forecasts about three-quarters to a full year ahead of the actual retail market season. For example, the spring/summer apparel color forecasts for 1974 are available in early spring of 1973. Seems odd to you, who can turn on a dime, but remember, the bigger you get the slower you get. Rapid speed and instant mobility are two of the very few strong points you have when you are just starting out.

Women's apparel and the "me too" field of children's wear have the most detailed forecasts since their merchandising and designing are so strongly related to trends. Men's apparel is beginning to rely more on trendy fashion for sales impetus and this is reflected in the scope of the available forecasts. Home furnishings, with a much slower, more long-range selling pattern are less involved in current trends. Once a trend is established in home furnishings it will be around for a goodly length of time before it is ousted in favor of something really new and different.

To send for copies of the current color and trend forecasts write a short note on your business stationery if you have any, stating that you are a designer in whatever field you work in, and that you would like to receive a copy of the color and trend forecast for your specific field. Be as definite as you can. No one is going to send womenswear, menswear and home furnishings data out in response to a very general letter. If you want an answer, ask for exactly what you need. The information is gratis, of course, and you do not need to include a stamped, self-addressed envelope. A few of the companies and councils offering really outstanding material are listed in Appendix III, page 209.

FABRIC LIBRARIES

Fabric libraries are another source of great free information about coming trends, but are only available on the trade level if you happen to live near one of the three major merchandising centers: New York City, Los Angeles or Dallas.

The libraries, maintained by fiber companies and fiber councils, are pretty much restricted to apparel to date. The collections consist of groups of swatches and materials that are considered pace-setting for the coming seasons. They are compiled by the fashion and marketing staffs of the company or council, who survey the fabric and material manufacturers and select things they feel are important in light of what has been happening in the past, and what seems to be taking shape in Europe and other trend-setting areas.

The swatches and samples are often grouped for

display on large bulletin boards, to illustrate a trend or a direction. For example, when plaids and prints were being first shown as complementary patterns for use in one and the same garment, every fabric library in town featured a board of "Complementaries."

Designers and editors who visit the libraries are given the names and ordering information for any fabrics they see that they like. Then, when the season rolls around, the fiber company has a pretty good idea of who is using its fiber, and thus, who is available to promote and publicize. (No, you will probably not be smothered with offers of free publicity—at least until you have built your name up into being a pace-setting new designer.) For more information on fabric libraries write to any of the companies or councils listed in Appendix III, page 209.

Many of the larger museums and design schools maintain excellent fabric libraries. The theme of these collections is usually in showing fabric trends in a historical perspective, and as such will lack up-to-the-minute data. Obviously you can't depend on these collections to show you what fabrics you can purchase, but regular use of the museum-type libraries will bring you a broader approach to the materials you work with, and you will be better able to shop the current market. Check your area to see what fabric libraries and collections are available to you.

TRADE PAPERS

Since the network of trade people is relatively small in proportion to consumers, and since mass distribution brings products from every part of the world into American stores, it is vital that you keep yourself informed of trends, marketing news, new raw materials, new creative influences and new designs. By reading the national trade newspapers regularly you build up an understanding of your field that cannot be achieved in any other manner. You begin to understand where and how "looks" or design areas begin and end and how each part of a field relates to the whole. You "learn" the "language."

You can begin to follow an influence, see it develop and expand, and decide whether or not you want to include it in your work. For example, Nixon's trip to China heralded vast Chinese influence in American apparel and home furnishings design. This influence was predicted early on, interpreted and fully reported in the trade papers. Had you been designing a commercial line at the time you might have put in a few items reflecting that trend, as indicated to you by the trade press. Coverage such as this, directed specifically to trade persons, cannot be found in any other group of publications.

Another example is the coverage of the plans already being drafted for 1976 to celebrate the two hundredth birthday of the United States. Each state will have its own fiesta; the promotion possibilities boggle the mind. Multitudes of apparel and home furnishings products will be sold relative to the celebration, most of which will be reported and/or sketched in the trade press long before they appear on the consumer market. It might be beneficial to you to get in on this—think eagles and stars and read your trade paper!

The first cache of information you need to know about is Fairchild Publications, Inc., publishers of major trade newspapers for women's apparel (*Women's Wear Daily*), men's apparel (*Daily News Record*), and home furnishings (*Home Furnishings Daily*.) If you are seriously in the business you will most probably end up reading one of the Fairchild papers. In the major market areas the papers are sometimes found on newsstands, but the usual way to make sure you get your trade news is to subscribe. However, each day of the week a certain segment of each field is covered in depth, and Fairchild very nicely offers partial subscriptions for people who are interested only in a specific topic.

Women's Wear Daily offers daily coverage on fabrics, dresses, coats, suits, all-weather wear, rainwear, financial news, and sportswear. Their special daily in-depth coverage schedule is as follows:

> *Monday:* Children's wear, computer technology, fabric technology, sportswear fashion news
> *Tuesday:* Display and packaging, maternity, furs, home sewing, sportswear market news
> *Wednesday:* Sportswear
> *Thursday:* Intimate apparel, loungewear, sportswear market and fashion news (greeting cards and stationery—second Thursday of each month)
> *Friday:* Cosmetics, millinery, gloves, handbags, hosiery, jewelry, wigs, all other main floor accessories

Women's Wear Daily offers complete subscriptions for the full week, or subscriptions for any one specific day, Monday through Friday. The address is: Women's Wear Daily, 7 East 12th Street, New York, New York 10003.

Home Furnishings Daily has daily coverage on all news in the home furnishings industry. The special daily in-depth coverage schedule is:

> *Monday:* Furniture, bedding, lamps and accessories

Tuesday: Floor coverings
Wednesday: Major appliances, home entertainment
   systems
Thursday: Housewares and electric housewares
Friday: Home textiles, curtains, draperies, linens,
   tablewares (Bath shop, alternate Fridays)

Home Furnishings Daily offers complete full-week subscriptions or once-a-week partial subscriptions for Mondays, Tuesdays and Fridays. Write to: Home Furnishings Daily, 7 East 12th Street, New York, New York 10003.

Daily News Record has daily coverage on all phases of the textile and men's and boy's wear industries. Also included are industrial textiles and government supply news. In-depth coverage of various segments of these fields is offered on certain days but no partial subscriptions are offered at present. Complete full-week subscriptions are available from: Daily News Record, 7 East 12th Street, New York, New York 10003.

If you decide you simply do not need to subscribe to a newspaper even on a partial subscription you may still be able to benefit from the very knowledgeable Fairchild news coverage of women's apparel. *Women's Wear Daily* is syndicated to a number of major newspapers in various parts of the country. By following these "local" papers you can keep track of the Paris collections, trends and other news of the trade. There is usually a credit line listing *Women's Wear Daily* as the source for reprinted articles, so watch for fashion reprints in:

Chicago *Tribune,* Chicago, Illinois
Cleveland *Press,* Cleveland, Ohio
Houston *Post,* Houston, Texas
Oakland *Press,* Pontiac, Michigan
Philadelphia *Inquirer,* Philadelphia, Pennsylvania

Rochester *Democrat and Chronicle,* Rochester, New
    York
Rochester *Times Union,* Rochester, New York
San Francisco *Chronicle,* San Francisco, California
Seattle *Times,* Seattle, Washington

Another division of Fairchild Publications that might
be helpful for reference material is the Books & Visual
Department, which publishes technical trade books.
Titles include: *Patterngrams—How to Copy Designs at
Home, Ceramics for the Table, Children's Wear De-
sign,* and *World of Furs.* If you are interested in build-
ing up a basic business library for yourself, write for the
Books and Visuals catalogs, which list available topics
and have directions for ordering single copies by mail.
The address is: Books & Visuals Dept. CM, Fairchild
Publications, Inc., 7 East 12th Street, New York, New
York 10003.

So much for Fairchild Publications. Two smaller
publishing companies, California Fashion Publications
and Fashion Week, Inc., both located in Los Angeles,
put out regional trade publications covering the West
Coast apparel industries. If you are located in the West,
selling in Western markets, you might find reading the
regional press more beneficial to you than getting your
national news out of New York City. However, it is
wise to look at everything that is available to you before you send for a subscription.

California Apparel News offers complete coverage on
all women's and children's apparel and accessories.
California Stylist has complete coverage on men's and
boy's apparel and accessories. For information on both
the above, write to: California Fashion Publications,
1011 South Los Angeles Street, Los Angeles, California
90015.

Fashion Week is a weekly newspaper covering all women's and children's apparel and accessories. *Men's Week* comes out every other week and covers all men's and boy's apparel and accessories. For information on both of the above, write: Fashion Week, Inc., 1016 South Broadway Place, Los Angeles, California 90015.

TRADE MAGAZINES AND NEWSLETTERS

Other important parts of the trade press are the many and varied special interest publications devoted to specific segments of the crafts field. Keeping up with new developments in your field should be a regular part of your work week, not to be postponed under any circumstances. You may never in your life copy someone else's design but you, like the rest of us, are affected by everything you encounter. So make sure you encounter your trade press on a regular basis and give yourself the benefit of the creative stimulation that is readily available to you.

Locating your specific trade press and selecting which of the many periodicals are most beneficial to you can be a problem, especially if you are in a rural area. Accept the fact that a field simply does not exist that does not have a trade publication. It's just a matter of ferreting them out. A consultation with your local librarian will be helpful, plus inquiries made to your suppliers. If you can't actually get hold of a copy of the magazine or newsletter to look over before you subscribe, write to the editor/publisher and see if you can get a single edition by mail.

A partial listing of the names and addresses of better trade publications can be found in Appendix IV, page 210.

chapter VI

Bookkeeping, Accounting, and Other Financial Considerations

SETTING UP YOUR BOOKS

At the words "accounting" and "bookkeeping" many designers' eyes glaze over and their attention evaporates rapidly. Which is pretty silly because if there is one thing you don't have to worry about it is accounting and bookkeeping. Somewhere along the line a mystique has developed, complete with mental pictures of dusty, Dickensian figures poring over stacks of ledgers. Relax. That's not going to be you.

The basic function of bookkeeping is to keep a record of what has happened to the business in the past. Each day's transactions are noted, and the history of that specific business is compiled. In a sense the records are the personal diary of the company. Accurate books are required so they can prove without a doubt exactly what went on each day the business operated. In case of differences of opinion regarding amounts of taxes owed to the government, a business's records are used to trace the ebb and flow of taxable materials. Or, if stockholders of a corporation question income or expenses of a business, the books are sent for and are used to document any and all claims. Books are accepted as the decisive word in all disputes.

Happily, the law doesn't require any particular system for keeping books. But the law does require that adequate records must be kept by every business. So between those two extremes you have a lot of latitude— enough so you can find a system that works for you.

The easiest way for the beginning craftsperson to set up an adequate system is to purchase two school notebooks and mark one INCOME and the other EXPENSES. Once you've done that you have set up your bookkeeping system. Now all you have to do is fill in the blank pages.

Each business day keep the notebooks handy. In the EXPENSE book jot down a notation of every cent you pay out, including taxi or bus fare, stamps or parcel post charges, light bulbs, gasoline—everything you spend that day for your business. Be really scrupulous about this because things get all mixed up if you don't make notes and suddenly you realize you've spent every cent in your wallet and you didn't quite remember what it all went for. Most demoralizing.

In the INCOME notebook jot down everything you take in from any source each day. This is generally much easier to remember than what you spent on taxi fare. With all entries either in the INCOME or EXPENSES book include the date, and be sure to write legibly. Milton E. Maybruck, head of the New York accounting firm of the same name, maintains that legibility is one of the main difficulties with owner-kept small-business books. If you can't read your writing or remember what your own shorthand abbreviations translate back to, your bookkeeping system is of minimal value.

INVOICES

Closely tied in with bookkeeping are your invoices, the bills you send out to buyers of your crafts. If you are selling direct to the consumer, i.e., retailing your own things, chances are you won't be making out a standard invoice. Stationery stores carry books of receipt forms such as you get from smaller stores when you make a purchase. Fill in your business name and address on the top of the form, or if you have had a rubber stamp made, stamp your name and address on the top of the form and you are ready to sell.

Retailing also means you will have to charge the sales taxes, if any, levied by your state, county, city or town. Be sure you understand what the taxes are and how you figure them out. After you get these facts under control it is a real help to make up a chart of the amount of tax per dollar you must charge, and keep this chart in the same place as your invoice book. Then when you make a sale you don't have to go through the agonies of mathematics to take the percentages of your totals. Keep copies of all the receipts you issue so you can transfer the record of the sale into your INCOME book accurately.

A side benefit of the receipt book is that you can utilize it to build up a permanent customer mailing list. When you make the receipt ask for the customer's name and address. Stash your copies of the receipts away, and the next time you have made up a new line, or have had a publicity write-up (see Chapter X: Publicity and Promotion) get out all the receipts and address envelopes or cards from the names and addresses. It's helpful if you make a note of the purchase date so you can discard the receipts that are over a year old, thus keeping your mailing list current. If you are selling direct to the consumer it's surprising how much business results from periodic personalized mailings inviting past customers back to see your new things.

If you are wholesaling, the invoice takes on a whole new importance. It is not only the bill you send to retailers who have purchased from you; it is also a statement of what you understand are the terms of the sale, protecting you from claims above and beyond what you spell out on the invoice. Your invoice is in there fending off disaster for you.

Aside from the business name, address and telephone number, complete with zip and area codes, a number is placed at the top of each invoice sheet. Since invoices are issued in duplicate or triplicate, be sure to allow enough copies having the same number for everyone. In the beginning you will probably just type out the invoices yourself. Eventually if you start to do enough business you will want to duplicate or mimeograph a form, perhaps the one included in this chapter. If so, leave the invoice number space blank and fill it in yourself when you make up the invoices. Then there will be no mix-up on duplicates and triplicates.

Below your name and number you list "Sold To" and also "Shipped To." Fill in the complete name and address of the buyer, and of the place you actually delivered the merchandise to, which is often a warehouse outside of the high-rent retailing district. This is an important protection for you to have in writing. If by some chance the shipment went astray you can begin tracing it not only through your carrier but also from the receiving end. "Shipped via" is another bit of protection and should be filled in in detail in case tracing is necessary.

Next is a simple statement that "Returns or damage claims are not accepted unless made within 5 days after Receipt of Merchandise." This is crucial. Unscrupulous retailers too often take advantage of the naive new business person and accept a shipment, put it out in the store, wait a few weeks and if it doesn't sell they pack it up and send it back to the designer with a vague note about the sizing being not what they had expected or the colors not the same shade they believed they had ordered, or some other trumped-up excuse. In reality the retailer did not "buy" the goods at all, but merely borrowed them, leaving the designer holding the bag when a box of tired, shopworn merchandise arrives back, unpaid-for and unusable. It's one thing to agree to "consignment" but another thing to be misled and duped.

Then comes a statement of your terms. Looking back on it, it took me months to understand terms, but after I caught on they were a big help to me. Terms have many uses. They are a statement of the several ways you will accept payment for the goods the buyer has ordered. If the buyer will pay right away he can take a bit of money off the total bill as sort of a reward for good behavior. If the buyer makes you wait a long time for your money then he will have to pay every cent that the bill states. In case this sounds a bit arbitrary let me say that you and the buyer agree on terms when the order is being placed, long before you make up the invoice.

Most common terms are stated as 2% 10 Net 30. Decoded this means that your buyer can deduct 2 percent from the total bill if he sends you the money within ten days. If he waits longer than ten days he must send you the full amount, and if he really drags his feet and waits until after the thirty days you are going to start nagging him for the money and perhaps even refuse to sell him anything else.

When dealing with big stores you generally must go along with whatever they use as their regular terms even though you are the term-setter theoretically. No giant retailer is going to change his normal payment procedure for one small resource. But the payment terms that you and the buyer will agree on almost always come down to something in the neighborhood of 2% 10 Net 30.

Next on your invoice is the listing and description of exactly what was ordered and the price you and the buyer agreed on per item. It is in your best interest to make this section as detailed and as specific as possible so no uncertainty remains about which style number was ordered in what quantities and in what colors and at what price. Again, advantage is too often taken of the unknowing newcomer, and if a retailer wants to return goods that didn't sell he will look through the invoice to see if he can spot some vagueness in wording to base his return claim on. Don't let it happen!

Total up the money owed you, send the packages off and then add the shipping charges to the price of the goods in order to get a Total Invoice Amount. Once in a great while a retailer will have some system for picking up merchandise, but usually you put out the money for the postage and insurance or delivery charges, and then add that amount to the bill so you can be reimbursed. The Total Invoice Amount is the sum the payment check should be for, minus the discounted percentage if the bill is paid within the discount line. If the amount of the check differs, make a photocopy of your copy of the invoice and send it, with a covering letter, to the Accounting Department of the store if it is a large one, and direct to the proprietor if it's a smaller shop. In most large department stores the buyer is so far removed from the accounting people that you lose a lot of time if you send correspondence about mis-payments to the buyer.

The last thing on the invoice is a notation of who has copies of the bill—Original to customer, Copy for your business. You might decide to send a third carbon copy of the invoice along instead of a receipt, to be signed by the person who accepts the merchandise at the store. Naturally you want a receipt since it removes the possibility that the store might claim the order never came in when it actually was taken in and then misplaced or lost. Whether you decide to use a carbon of the invoice or a separate little receipt slip is up to you. Whichever way, it is a good idea to save those signature papers until after the bill is paid and the check is cleared just in case. See Invoice Form, page 75.

FIRE INSURANCE

Another thing you should be aware of when setting up your own business is insurance. There are two kinds, one of which is mandatory, and the other of which it may be smart to have anyhow. The non-required insurance is fire insurance on the raw materials you have purchased for the business. If you find you have accumulated a good-sized stock, plus some machinery or tools, you should think about taking out some fire insurance. Policies, rates and terms of insurance vary so

INVOICE FORM

Invoice # _____

Your Name
Address
Telephone No.

Date _____

Sold To   *Shipped To*
Name _____   _____
Address _____   _____
City _____   _____
  Shipped via:

Terms: 2% 10 Net 30   Returns or damage claims
                             not accepted unless made
                             within 5 days after Receipt
                             of Mdse.

Quantity   *Description*   *Unit Price*   *Total*

Total $ _____
Shipping Charges   _____
Total Invoice   ════════

Original to customer
Copy for you
Copy to Be Used as Receipt

widely in different parts of the country that no general statement is possible. When you feel that your business possessions merit insuring, call several insurance agents, have them come and give you estimates, and then select the arrangement that is the most beneficial to you. As in making most purchases, always shop around a bit before buying!

WORKMAN'S COMPENSATION AND DISABILITY

The mandatory insurance is Workman's Compensation and Disability. This is a two-headed program that had its beginnings in the Progressive Labor Movement in the early 1900s. Now each state has its own special way Workman's Compensation is handled, but the basic concept of insurance for working people is the core of each state's program. Workman's Compensation guarantees each worker an income of sorts if he is injured while on the job. This is not restricted to accidents that happen while in the office or studio; it also covers accidents that occur while traveling on business. The employer pays for the total amount of Workman's Compensation Insurance in New York State.

Disability, the handmaiden of Compensation, guarantees the worker an income of sorts if he is ill or injured while off the job, in his non-work hours, and is thus unable to work. Both the worker and the employer contribute to the cost of Disability Insurance in New York State. Small amounts of money are withheld from the worker's paycheck and funds are added to the withheld money by the employer, making up the necessary payments.

If your business is an individual proprietorship you

will not have to think about Workman's Compensation and Disability since you are the owner of the business, not the worker. True, you may be doing the worker tasks along with the management tasks, but technically you are the employer, not the employee. If you find you have to hire a worker, then you have to participate in Workman's Compensation and Disability. Since the interpretation of the plan varies from state to state write to the Department of Labor in your state, addressing the letter to that office in your capital city. Ask for information and the necessary forms to participate in the plan.

One last comment on Workman's Compensation. If you have established your business as a corporation rather than an individual proprietorship or a partnership you must have Workman's Compensation and Disability from the beginning. Even if you are the lone person involved in the business you are technically the worker hired by the corporation to run the business. So you are an employee and must, by law, be covered by the mandatory insurance.

LEASES

You should know a few facts about leases when you establish your place of business. Chances are you are working out of your home. Homes are usually in areas zoned as residential, prohibiting the encroachment of business enterprises. So be discreet when and if your sales volume begins to build. The neighbors will be admiring and supportive at your first business successes. But if they begin to feel that you are changing the neighborhood's character with delivery vans, workers and so forth, they could make trouble for you.

Be even more discreet if you are living and working in rented quarters. The usual residential lease prohibits working in the living area, so by carrying on your business from your home you are violating the terms of your lease and could be evicted if the building owner saw fit. Or you could be asked to leave or negotiate a new lease, since commercial space usually rents for more than residential space.

CASH FLOW

A wholesaling process you should know about is "cash flow." This is the manner in which your money comes in and goes out. Not how much you are making or what you are doing with it, simply the track record of your business. The reason that cash flow assumes any importance at all is that the pace and timing of your money movements make life serene and happy if they work right and will drive you crazy if they don't.

For example, when you start your business you need a lump sum of money to spend on your supplies, transportation, telephone, stationery, packing materials, postage and other essentials. These might be minuscule amounts if you are beginning modestly, but you still need ready cash to cover them.

So you get the money together and spend it on the necessary items. Then it takes you about a month to make up your line and to sell it, using the terms 2% 10 Net 30. Unless you have taken the precaution to have a certain amount of cash stashed away for day-to-day expenses while you are waiting out the ten days or the thirty days, or God forbid even longer, you are in trouble. Without cash you can't go out and buy more supplies, get into the market, make phone calls, make up more items and show and sell them. In reality you needed money to carry you for two months, not just the first thirty days. True, you made your sales and the money is coming in but the fact that it hasn't arrived yet is what is wrong.

Add to this example incidentals like checks getting lost in the mail, incorrect payment amounts, insufficient funds, and you would be wiped out even further in your timing. The conclusion to reach here is that at least three months' worth of money is the safest amount to aim for. Figure out your money needs and multiply by three or better yet, by four. Squirrel it away in your separate bank account if it's a small enough amount so that you don't have to borrow. And if you do have to borrow, do it well in advance so you won't end up strapped for the amount of time it takes for a loan to come through.

If you find your cash flow is not working right for you an adjustment can sometimes be made by rearranging the terms you and your buyers settle on. Smaller shops will often be willing to cooperate and pay you sooner than your regular terms indicate, understanding that you are small and just starting out. The inference here is, of course, that once you get everything under control they can go back to your regular terms.

If nobody seems inclined to be a good guy and help you out then you can offer to change your terms and let them discount 4 percent and 5 percent on bills paid within the week. Just make sure they understand that it is only a temporary arrangement and will be abandoned as soon as possible. This type of terms-changing can come in handy whenever you need quick cash and your money cupboard is bare. A few phone calls can often scare up cash that same day if the discount percentages are attractive enough!

BANK LOANS

There is some basic data on bank loans you should know about. You may never use it, but it's a good idea to be aware of the kind of arrangements that are most commonly made by banks to lend money. First off, the words "to lend money" are something of a misnomer. Loaning is simply borrowing and paying back exactly what you borrow. A bank loan seems to me to be more of a rental situation. You rent the use of a sum of money from the bank. When you are finished with the money you return it and pay the rental fee, which is called interest. Looked on this way, the role of a bank in the business community is more clearly understood.

Banks are in business to lend or rent money. That's what they make a lot of their profit from. Of course they are going to be selective about whom they rent their money to, just as you are selective about whom you sell your designs to. Banks check out every detail of the loan applications they receive to try and be sure their money will be returned on time and the rental fee/interest will be paid in full.

In order to seriously interest a bank in lending you some money you have to present it with a detailed picture of your business. This wipes out the possibility of getting a bank loan to set yourself up in a new business. Generally a bank will need to know your business history in order to judge whether or not it will grant you a loan. It will want information in four specific areas:

1: The source of your money to date

2: Data on your products, including costing sheets and a description of where you fit into the market and your competitive situation

3: Some idea of the timing of your business, the cash flow as indicated by your INCOME and EXPENSES notebooks

4: Concrete plans on how you expect to pay the loan money back to the bank.

Lending procedures vary in different parts of the country and for different industries. However, some general facts seem to hold true. There are only two types of bank loans you need to know about. One is a Direct Loan, also called a Demand or Time Note. With this type of loan you get the use of the money for a set amount of time, usually ninety days, or payable on demand. These loans are difficult to get and require an outstanding business record, plus security.

Security for this type of loan narrows down to whatever can be converted back into hard cash easily and quickly. For example, stocks, bonds, savings account passbooks, and some life insurance policies are considered acceptable as security. Among the lengthy list of items not usable as security are cars, jewelry, boats, homes and land. This might seem odd since these things are certainly of definite value. Still, banks feel they are not knowledgeable on the day-to-day values and are unwilling to deal in these areas.

The other kind of bank loan is the Monthly Payment Loan, also called an Installment Loan. These are much easier to come by, and may be considered for a relatively new business venture. In this type of loan the bank will match you dollar for dollar. You put up half the cash and the bank puts up the other half. In addition you often must guarantee personally that you will be responsible for the repayment even if the business goes bankrupt. The loan is life-insured too, so the bank will be repaid even if something terrible happens to you. All in all, the risk to the bank is far less with the Monthly Installment Loan, and therefore more easily granted.

If the bank is reluctant to grant you the Monthly Installment Loan you might suggest bringing in a Guarantor, some person with money and/or good credit who says he will be responsible for the repayment of the money in case you default. If you can't think of anybody to be a Guarantor you can suggest that the bank loan officer consider applying to the Small Business Administration to guarantee your loan. (See Chapter III: Where to Go for Professional Advice.)

Sometimes a bank will offer to grant you a portion of the loan you applied for. It might be hesitant about the entire amount but still feel that your application is a good one. If this happens ask the loan officer to go over the entire thing with you so you can have the benefit of his thinking about which areas he feels are less strong than others. He deals in loan applications every day and might be able to tell you things you are doing or things you are planning that could be handled in a different and better way. It is smart to listen to any constructive criticism and consider changes that would make your operation more acceptable as a business risk.

A last word on banks—be sure to shop around and check several banks if you possibly can before you actually take out a loan. Not only do you want to find *simpatico* people to do business with, but each bank usually has slightly different arrangements on loans, payments and so forth, even though the interest rates might be identical. Find one that works well for you. Remember, the bank will be making money on your loan so if you aren't pleased with what one bank offers you, just take your business elsewhere!

INCOME TAX

Now how about your own income tax if you are in business for yourself? The money you make or lose in your business is of interest to the federal, state and local tax departments. You will be expected to keep everybody informed of your situation.

Each tax department in each portion of the government—federal, state and local—has established a figure that represents the lowest amount of money you can earn in one year and still be taxed. For example—in 1973 in the United States (federal tax level) you could earn up to $2,050 before you had to bother about paying federal income tax.

This figure is changeable, and may or may not coincide with the figures established by state and local tax bureaus. So step number one is to write to the federal, state and local tax bureaus and request complete information, including how to figure depreciation (more on this later), partial use of your home, automobile, telephone, etc., for business. The federal tax form that covers all this is Form 1040 Schedule C, which basically reports your individual profit and loss.

Gather in all available information and explanatory pamphlets and see what you can do with them. Tax preparation is complicated, and, in a way, highly personal. You might feel confident about tackling it yourself. Or you might decide to consult an accountant who would be conversant with the subtleties of tax law.

If you do decide on an accountant and don't know

anyone who can recommend one, call or write the nearest office of the National Association of Accountants and ask for recommendations of accountants who would be available to someone just starting out in business. Be sure you come to a clear understanding of the fee and time involved before you actually set up a work session. Accountants, like lawyers and doctors, charge for consulting.

DEPRECIATION

For tax purposes, when you buy a piece of equipment or machinery you are not supposed to consider the entire purchase price as an immediate expense since you expect the equipment to last for a while. Theoretically you are supposed to spread the expense over a number of years, until the equipment will be worn out and have to be replaced. The manner in which you write up this spreading out of expenses is referred to as "depreciation."

Since depreciation is a mind-boggling concept, it is best to deal in examples. Say, for example, you buy a machine that costs $500, and you fully expect this machine to last for ten years of normal use. True, you've paid out the $500, probably the day you bought it. But when you make out your taxes (Form 1040 Schedule C, for instance) you make reference to this whole situation, and then list $50 as your expense *this* year and every year until your estimated ten years of machine life has run out.

In other words, you divide the total cost of the equipment by the number of years you estimate it will last, and then put in the fractionalized share of the purchase price for each year of your time estimate.

The question of how you estimate the possible life of your equipment gets even murkier. The Federal Bureau of Internal Revenue issues a publication in which it lists suggested life spans for many types of equipment. If the question of depreciation comes up for you, by all means write for the booklet. But understand that it merely suggests possible guidelines, and you do not have to follow these guidelines unless you agree with them. You really have to work out your own set of wear life figures, and aim for what you hope will be a reasonable figure.

If you have purchased used equipment, the same drill holds, but used equipment is expected to have a much shorter wear life than new equipment. In fact, if you have purchased a really creaky old piece of equipment that you are sure will not last out the year, you are allowed to go back and list it on the tax form as an outright business expense of the year in which you bought it.

The instruction pamphlets you will receive from all the tax bureaus you write to will have more to say on the subject, and in a more positive manner.

chapter VII

Costing

This is the chapter that tells you how to figure out what to charge for your items in order to make a profit. As such it is probably the most important chapter in the book. If you cost your products correctly, produce and sell them regularly, you will be building up a good, sound business. And if you don't cost them correctly, whether or not you produce and sell them regularly becomes a moot point and the whole thing soon turns into a ghastly mess.

A good but terrible case in point is retailer Jimmi York's early adventure into the fur hat business. Jimmi, back before her retailing days, was making fur ski parkas out of old fur coats. A slice of fur was left over from each coat, so she designed and made up a big, longhaired fur hat. The year was 1959, and nobody was doing big fur hats, or much of anything else with longhaired furs. Jimmi, whose ability for recognizing a hot item is legendary, knew she had a winner in the hat.

Shortly after, Jimmi hired a furrier, bought up a batch of aging furs and opened up a fur hat division named Fur Flyers. As an ex-buying office employee she knew her way around New York merchandising circles, and figured she needed a quick blast of publicity to get Fur Flyers off the ground. *Glamour* magazine seemed like a logical place to try, so she made an appointment with the accessories editor who flipped as soon as Jimmi walked in with the hats.

Publicity was instantaneous. Every editor who saw the hats wanted one. The trade was alerted, buyers were contacted, and sales poured in. The much coveted front cover of the back-to-school issue of *Glamour* had a gorgeous color close-up of a model wearing a Fur Flyer hat. Eventually *Glamour* named the Fur Flyer hats their Accessory of the Year, and sent Jimmi a huge bouquet of long-stemmed red roses as a thank you.

Of course every furrier in town was knocking Jimmi off by then, but it was such a hot item there was plenty of business for all. The big Fur Flyer hat became the status symbol of that season. It seemed as if every store window that showed winter coats also showed the mannequins wearing big, longhaired fur hats. Other magazines, television and the newspapers picked up the item and featured it coast to coast.

Jimmi became a celebrity overnight also, and was written up, photographed and interviewed. "It was like the second coming," said Jimmi. All she had to do was to enjoy herself and make sure the supply of old fur coats kept flowing into the loft where her staff of furriers pulled them apart and remade the skins into hats.

But unfortunately she had done her costing wrong. She had figured three complete hats out of each ancient coat. The sad reality turned out to be two hats per old coat. This mistake compounded itself as the sales volume increased, and Jimmi found herself in serious trouble. She also found herself in the curious position of being the toast of the New York market at the same time she was declaring bankruptcy to her creditors. (These things always sound so funny in retrospect, but it wasn't a bit amusing when it happened.)

Jimmi, sadder but wiser, went on to become what she is today, the co-owner of "Bedlam" and "Fancy That," exciting and successful New York boutiques. So the story has a happy ending, but the point about the importance of costing is well taken.

Now, as to your own costing methods—understand that the first few times you figure out costs it will take you ages. But fortunately it isn't always like that. After you catch on, the costing procedure becomes less and less confusing until you can almost do it in your head. And as you figure the costs of many items or lines you will become less and less personally involved in the process until it becomes just another business procedure with the same emotional content as sealing an envelope!

I have never met a new designer/craftsperson who did not have an overabundance of personal feeling about costing his line. Everybody seems to fall into two groups. One group feel that no matter how much they charge it will never be enough to reward them for their creative effort. The other group feel, equally fervently, that any amount they ask will be too much to ask in return for their creative effort. Notice that the real value of the product involved does not figure in either of these loony rationales.

So expect to be a little nutty about costing. Nuttiness is all right, but not inaccuracy. Ignore the disquieting inner voice, get out a pencil and paper, and begin to apply the formulas. It all works out. And if you don't like the answer you come up with there are four places you can doctor up a bit to try and get results you feel more comfortable with.

There are four major categories to deal with when you cost an item:

Direct Material Costs
Direct Labor Costs
Overhead Expenses
Profit You Want to Make

DIRECT MATERIAL COSTS

Let's discuss direct material costs first. The direct material costs simply mean the total sum of everything you have to use to make up your item. Direct material costs include every tiny scrap of material, every whiff of spray or finish, every last sequin. They do not include the boxes you ship in, the cord, labels, etc. Simply the raw materials, that's all.

Since you need to list every little thing that goes into your item it generally works out to be easier to figure an entire group of items and then divide back to find the cost per item. The type of group you figure out will have to depend on you, your products and your timing. I usually try to figure on the basis of a half dozen, a dozen, a gross, or so many per hour, per day or per week. Then you are able to say how much glue you've used (an ounce?) and how much thread you've sewn (a spool?) or how many rhinestones are set in.

Say for example you are sewing skirts that take one and a half yards of fabric per skirt, and you can produce three skirts per day. Some skirts are made out of fabric costing $1.00 a yard, and others are made from fabric costing $2.00 per yard. The same pattern is used for the $1.00-a-yard and the $2.00-a-yard skirts, and you want to figure out the costing for both.

Begin your Direct Material Costs sheet by listing two columns, one for the $1.00-a-yard fabric and the other for the $2.00-a-yard fabric. The normal work week is five days. If you sew three skirts each day for five days, your week's production is fifteen skirts. You know your skirt pattern calls for one and a half yards for each skirt. So set it up this way:

	Fabric Cost *$1.00 per yd.*	*Fabric Cost* *$2.00 per yd.*
Fabric for one week's production, i.e., 15 skirts @ 1½ yds. per skirt = 22½ yds. per week	$22.50	$45.00

The fabric is only the outer part of the skirt. Next you must figure your lining, your interfacing, stiffening or other hidden fabric uses. And make the next entry on your Direct Material Costs sheet:

Linings, interfacing, stiffening, etc., 50¢ per skirt x 15 skirts per week	$7.50	$7.50

Now theoretically you've finished with the basic fabrics. Start to count up the zippers, snaps, buttons, hooks and eyes or other hardware that is "behind the scenes" in making a skirt. Your next Direct Material Costs sheet entry will be:

Zipper, buttons, snaps,
etc., 50¢ per skirt x 15
skirts per week $7.50 $7.50

Possibly you are dressing the skirt up a bit with
a belt, a clasp, or some other ornament, using a more
expensive version on the more expensive fabric. So list
them:

Belts, ornaments:
50¢ per skirt x 15
75¢ per skirt x 15 . . . . $7.50 $11.25

The final item on the Direct Material Costs sheet
should cover all the other tiny but vital materials such
as thread, seam binding, elastic, etc. Be as accurate as
you can be on these:

Thread, binding, etc.,
one week's supply $5.00 $5.00

If you have anything left over that goes into your
skirts as raw material and that hasn't been accounted
for, list it. Then total up the two columns and you will
find out what the raw materials are costing you to make
up a week's worth, i.e., fifteen finished skirts. You'll see
in our example that you need to put out $50.00 worth
of material for fifteen $1.00-per-yard skirts, and you
need to put out $76.25 for fifteen skirts made from the
$2.00-per-yard fabric. (See *Costs Sheet,* page 92.)

DIRECT LABOR COSTS

Put that sheet aside and title the next page Direct
Labor Costs sheet. This one will be a lot shorter, but
might be harder to put together. Most probably you,
as the new business person, are making up the products

Direct Material Costs Sheet

Direct Cost— Materials	Fabric Cost $1.00/yd.	Fabric Cost $2.00/yd.
Fabric for 1 week's production: 15 skirts @ 1½ yds. each = 22½ yds. @ cost per yd.	$22.50	$45.00
Linings, interfacings etc.: 50¢ per skirt x 15 skirts	7.50	7.50
Zippers, buttons, snaps: 50¢ per skirt x 15 skirts	7.50	7.50
Belts, ornaments, etc. 50¢ per skirt x 15 skirts 75¢ per skirt x 15 skirts	7.50	11.25
Thread, seam binding, etc., one week's supply	5.00	5.00
TOTAL DIRECT MATERIAL COST	$50.00	$76.25

yourself. You have no staff of workers. But you are also the designer of the items, and the owner of the business, if not to say the seller, bookkeeper, secretary, and the anything-else-that-needs-to-be-done person. If the business prospers you will want and need to hire skilled hands to replace yours in actually making up the products to be shipped each day. These skilled hands are going to cost you money—a definite salary per day, hour or week, or by the piece, the dozen or the gross.

In order to make up an accurate Direct Labor Costs

sheet you must find out how much you would need to pay to a skilled craftsperson who would replace you in duplicating the items you have designed. You might have to check newspapers to see what the going rates are for sewing machine operators, or leather workers or whatever your field is. Perhaps you know somebody who would be able to make professional duplicates of your line if you supplied him with the materials. Keep in mind the minimum wage laws and figure out an approximate weekly salary that you would have to pay somebody to produce the necessary number of products.

You probably feel you are light years away from ever hiring another person. You still need an accurate figure so you can correctly establish your costs. Unless your product is so completely individual that you could never replace your own skilled hands, you must poke around and come up with a salary figure for a worker. I have never had too much patience with designers who claim that it would be impossible to ever hire anyone to duplicate their works. Even the Great Renaissance masters like Michelangelo and da Vinci had rooms full of workers dutifully turning out cupids and draperies by the yard which were then passed off as done by The Man himself.

So on your Direct Labor Costs sheet you might have a listing such as:

Worker, salary for one week $100.00

Now add this figure to both the Direct Material Costs total for the $1.00-per-yard skirt and to the Direct Material Costs total for the $2.00-per-yard skirt. You will see that you must spend for *materials plus labor* $150.00 per week to make up the fifteen finished skirts from the $1.00-per-yard fabric, and $76.25 per week to make up the fifteen skirts from the $2.00-per-yard fabric.

Which means, dividing it all back down to find the cost per skirt, that each one of the less expensive fabric skirts is costing you $10.00 in materials and labor, and each one of the more expensive fabric skirts is costing you $11.75 in materials and labor.

OVERHEAD EXPENSES

Your costing is now half completed. The next expense you have to figure out is your overhead. You really have to be scrupulously honest about overhead. It's so easy to slip up by saying that you are working in a corner of the garage so you really don't have any rent, and the telephone is used by the whole family so you really don't have any phone bill, and so on. But the accuracy of your costing depends on estimating logical amounts for all categories of expenses.

As to rent, if you are working at home figure a portion of your total rent, in proportion to your work space and storage areas. If this is unfeasible check the newspapers and real estate listings for your neighborhood and figure out what it would cost you to rent a small work area if you needed to. Pick a general, middle-of-the-road imaginary rent figure. If most of the area lofts rent for $100.00 per month, list it. True, you might luck into a great work space at half that price, but all you need for your Overhead Expenses sheet is a typical cost figure.

Gas and electricity bills must be figured out proportionately. Handwork seldom involves heavy machinery except for home kilns for firing ceramics, and the electric input is usually listed on the kiln. Count the number of lights and small appliances you use each work day, compare it to the total usage per month and you will be able to make an educated guess.

A good way to keep track of business phone calls is to keep a small pad next to the phone and mark down each outgoing call you make. Divide this into the total bill and you will have a pretty accurate figure.

Your packing and shipping supplies are considered overhead expenses, as are delivery and freight charges. Don't forget to include any tips you give regularly for special services. One company I dealt with often had a nasty delivery man who insisted his instructions were only to deliver the large bolts of fabric onto the sidewalk outside my building. If I wanted him to carry them inside to my workroom I would have to pay him extra. Pay him I did, although I always felt that "Sidewalk Delivery" was a gigantic rip-off. And Old Nasty's tip got counted into my overhead because I had to pay it regularly.

Your Overhead Expenses sheet might look like this:

Overhead Expense	Monthly Expense
Rent	$100.00
Electricity	24.00
Telephone	12.00
Insurance	15.00
Cleaning	20.00
Packing Materials & Supplies	15.00
Delivery and Freight	20.00
Office supplies, postage	10.00
Repairs and Maintenance	15.00
Payroll Taxes	5.00
Any Other Expenses	20.00
TOTAL MONTHLY OVERHEAD	$256.00

Overhead Per Skirt

   15 skirts per week x 4 (weeks) = 60 skirts per month

   60 skirts divided into \$256.00 = \$4.27 overhead per
skirt

You find that your total monthly overhead is \$256.00, and your overhead per skirt comes to \$4.27. So you add the \$4.27 on to the other cost-per-skirt figures you have on your other pages—the \$10.00 per skirt that the raw materials and labor cost you to make one skirt out of the \$1.00-per-yard fabric, and also the \$11.25 per skirt that the raw materials and labor cost you to make the skirt out of the \$2.00-per-yard fabric.

You then have two total costs:

TOTAL COST PER SKIRT @ \$1/yd \$14.27
TOTAL COST PER SKIRT @ \$2/yd 16.02

PROFIT FIGURES

Now you know what the base costs are. But how about the profit you would like to make on each skirt? That has to be tacked onto the cost per skirt so you won't end up just breaking even, or just making the worker's wages.

Everyone wants to make as much profit as he can while still being competitively priced. The tricky question is how much profit you can add onto your total cost figures without making your products seem out-priced to a buyer.

A good approach to the profit question is to take a long look at your line and then go out and check the stores you want to sell to. Get an idea of what prices are tagged onto items similar to yours. Going back to the skirts, if you know each skirt is costing you \$14.27

without any profit, go check the boutique skirt departments you want to deal with and see what kind of
money they are getting for your kind of skirt. Bear in
mind that the retailer generally doubles the wholesale
price on women's wearing apparel. For example, if you
charge $20.00 for an item, the retailer would mark it
$40.00, or most probably $39.95. So your $14.27 skirt,
without any profit, would already be selling for around
$30.00.

Look carefully at what's in the $35.00 retail range. If
your skirts look as if they could get $35.00 then you
could make $5.00 profit per skirt. If they look better,
more like the $40.00 retail skirts, then you could make
$10.00 profit on each skirt. (And if you were also the
worker who made up the skirts you would be getting
the $100.00 per week worker's salary too.)

Settle on a price you think would be effective for your
skirts bearing in mind that you aren't looking for vast
volume orders to begin with. If you end up feeling you
can make $5.00 profit per skirt, then add the $5.00 to
your total expense figure, and you would have correctly
priced your $1.00-a-yard skirt to sell to the buyer at
$19.27. And the $2.00-a-yard skirt would sell to the
buyer at $21.02. The straggling 27¢ and the 2¢ look a
bit odd to the professional so round them off to the
nearest 75¢ amount, i.e., $20.75 for the $2.00-a-yard
skirt, and $18.75 for the $1.00-a-yard skirt.

Following through on our example, your own personal profit from a week's work would be $75.00. Plus
the worker's salary if you did the actual work. All of
which makes $175.00, which is quite nice. Most de-
signers I know have continued to do some amount of
actual work even after their businesses are built up

enough to hire a worker. (Then the costing changes because the number of items produced per week is higher as two people are turning out more volume.)

REVISING COSTS

That's the bright side of the costing picture. The gloomy side is when you do your expense sheets, get the totals, go to the stores and find you are already overpriced even before you add on your profit. There are a number of changes you can make to bring your expenses down so you can be competitively priced and still make a pleasant profit.

First move is to see if you can reduce your raw materials costs. In the example of the skirts, can you get a better, lower price for any of the materials by buying from another manufacturer or by buying in slightly larger quantities? Can you substitute a less expensive fabric or lining? Or a more expensive fabric and increase the value of the entire garment so it will look like a much better skirt? How about a shorter zipper, fewer snaps, buttons, etc.? Will a narrower elastic or seam binding serve your purpose but cost less? If you arrange to pick up your orders will you save on delivery charges?

The next thing to check is your production method. Can you re-plan your cutting and sewing operations so you can produce more skirts per day? Or can you simplify the construction so that fewer cutting and sewing steps are necessary to turn out a finished garment?

If you still need more cost reducing moves consider redesigning the item into a less complex garment.

Would a pocket cut from the waste fabric scraps add enough to the over-all design to compensate for the removal of an expensive ornament or the use of a less expensive belt buckle?

Finally, could any of your overhead expenses be reduced? One quick way to save is to buy misprinted packing boxes—ones that some other company ordered and refused to accept because its name was wrong or something. These you can pick up for next to nothing, and I've never found the printing on a fresh, new box to make any difference on the wholesale level. Is your method of shipping and insuring as low in cost as possible?

Usually adjustments can be made to bring items into the area where profits can be recognized. Occasionally I've run across designers who are certain they cannot cost their products in the usual way since their products are so radically different they have nothing to compare to in order to reach an acceptable profit figure.

If your items seem to be unrelated to anything on the market think a step further back and deal with them on the level of what job or service they are supposed to do for the consumer. If you are making marvelous wall hangings of hitherto-uncombined materials you are still competing with standard, traditional wall hangings, and your products will be viewed alongside of whatever else is in the wall hanging department of any store you sell to. Sure, you have a new and different combination of materials. But your customer is still a person looking for something to put up on his wall. He has a limited amount of money to spend on decoration of his room. Your prices must relate to the marketplace.

TERMS DISCOUNTS

Your offer of terms, perhaps 2% 10 Net 30, should be considered when figuring your profit. No flat rule can be established since you have no way of estimating how many of your customers are going to take the discount.

If you are working toward a very definite lump sum of profit money that you hope to accumulate in a specific time period, you would be smart to increase your final, total price by 2 percent (or your term offer) to take care of the possible cash loss. For example, if you are trying to get money together to pay tuition, or a mortgage, i.e., a non-flexible sum, you need to know exactly what you can count on for profit.

If, on the other hand, you can afford to be a bit more flexible and keep your profit figure a tiny bit loose in the beginning, keep track of the number of customers actually taking the discount on a regular basis. If you find at the end of six months or a year that you have been done out of a goodly sum, then begin to add 2 percent or whatever onto your total price to compensate for the discount.

If this chapter seems terribly complicated and confusing at the first reading, go back over it step by step. As you become more comfortable with the process try to cost a few of your own things. You will find that you begin to design more with costing in mind. If you come up with a smashing handbag that takes all week to produce you will know that it cannot go into your line of $25.75 handbags. And you'll know instinctively that the handblown Venetian beads would look fabulous in your jewelry but are not feasible in your line of $15.75 accessories.

Once you cost out a whole line of items you have the option of balancing the profit of the line, taking a bit more profit on some items and less on others. This is perfectly legitimate, but don't overdo it. You might just find yourself with a lot of volume on the tiny-profit numbers, and very few orders on the big-profit items that are supposed to balance out the line. However, it is usually wise to offer a buyer a variety of prices. Most of the time the buyer will select a few low-price, a few medium-price, and one or two of the most expensive you have.

Your customers and retail store buyers will categorize you as producing designs in certain set price levels. They depend on you to show and sell them products they are looking for within certain definite price spans. Each department in a retail store has a price range built into it, such as budget dresses, better dresses, and so forth. If you get too far out of your known price range you will no longer be able to sell to those buyers with whom you have been doing business and have built up a reputation. You will have to go out and find a new set of buyers dealing in your new price range, almost beginning all over again.

Better devote your efforts to designing and producing great-looking things in one certain price range rather than jumping all over the market. Eventually you might find you want to branch out and open subdivisions of your company. These would enable you to make a variety of items in different price ranges. But don't play around during the first year or two. Get yourself established first.

chapter VIII

Purchasing and Manufacturing

PURCHASING

No matter what your craft is, there are only two ways to buy your materials—wholesale or retail. The wholesale price is roughly half of the retail price, and there is a big difference between the two ways of doing business.

THE WHOLESALER

The wholesaler is set up to supply customers who are planning to resell the material they have purchased, perhaps in some other shape or form or in some other quantity or package. As such, the wholesaler does not charge his customers any retail sales tax, but requires them to furnish him with copies of their resale tax exemption certificate, or their resale license permit number. (See Chapter II.)

The wholesaler deals in sizable quantities of merchandise and generally adheres to the rigid quantity standards accepted in his trade for sample orders and minimum orders. After you establish your business credit with the wholesaler you open an account and you receive periodic bills for the goods you purchase. As on your own invoice, the wholesaler usually lists his terms of payment—perhaps 2% 10 Net 30. The wholesaler does not mark down merchandise and have sales, but he often has close-outs, seconds and irregulars which may be money-saving for you.

THE RETAILER

The retailer, on the other hand, is set up to supply material to consumers who are planning to keep whatever they have bought, and have no intention of reselling any part of their purchases. As such the retailer charges the consumer retail sales tax if any is levied in his area. The retailer will sell as much or as little of his merchandise as the customer requests, within the limits of his pre-packaged goods.

The retailer generally expects to be paid the full price in cash at the time the purchase is made, or will accept national credit cards or open a personal charge account as a courtesy to the regular customer. No discounts are offered for prompt payment.

The retailer will have periodic sales and clear-aways during which portions of his regular stock will be marked down, often near to the wholesale price. Retailers occasionally deal in seconds and irregulars on a lower price level than their first quality goods, but even the seconds and irregulars have a built-in retail mark-up and thus would be more expensive than the off-quality goods available from a wholesaler.

As the new business person you will find it to your advantage to buy on both the wholesale and retail levels. You will gradually shift off into complete wholesale buying as your business increases, if you have chosen to get into duplicative selling rather than one-of-a-kind. If you have decided to produce only single designs and not to duplicate, you might end up always buying on the retail level to avoid quantity minimums and to broaden your area of potential suppliers, allowing you to purchase wonderful things wherever and whenever you come across them.

BUYING WHOLESALE

The retailer, when you buy from him, will be happy to have your business. The wholesaler, on the other hand, will most probably do his utmost to discourage you from pestering him, will try to get you to take your business elsewhere, and will repeatedly insist that it is costing him more to process your tiny orders than he makes in profit from dealing with you. Which is probably true in the beginning, and is a concept you must work hard to repudiate.

The problem is pretty simple: wholesalers are set up to do business in large quantities. You want to buy wholesale since it is necessary for costing your items properly and assures you of continuity of material. But you prefer not to buy in huge amounts.

If your wholesaler's salespeople are on a commission basis you will fast find that nobody wants to wait on you. Or you will be assigned to the newest, greenest recruit on the sales staff, the low man on the totem pole who can't pass you off to anybody else. You represent a gigantic loss of time to them, with minimal profit potential. So they will try to avoid doing business with you. And, equally fervently, you will try to coerce them into doing business with you.

Your main weapon is charm. And your secondary strength is the vague fear implanted in the wholesaler that you are the greatest designer ever born. If he seriously insults you and you become the overnight sensation dealing in millions, you will never even see his salespeople when they come knocking at your golden door. Not much to work with but at least it's a beginning.

Be ready for lots of arguments when you first try to establish yourself with wholesalers. Always offer to pay cash before delivery, and to pick up orders personally in the beginning. And know your credentials. One designer I know had her resale tax exemption certificate encased in plastic so she could carry it with her, ready to wave under the nose of any wholesaler who accused her of trying to buy wholesale illegitimately.

Be friendly, bright, witty and charming. It helps. Eventually you will find a supplier or two who will become interested, if not fascinated with your minuscule business and who will open tiny accounts for you and accept your shaky credit rating. Years later, when you are big and successful, each of your early suppliers will proudly claim that he set you up in business and taught you everything you know. Let them enjoy it!

LOCATING SUPPLIERS

Now, how do you find suppliers? Ms. Judy Glassman, author of an information-packed paperback book called *Craft Supplies of New York,* suggests a four-way approach:

First, check all trade publications and newsletters for advertising, classified sections, or resource mentions. If the suppliers are not fully identified, write a note to the editor asking for full name and addresses of companies in your field. Be as specific as possible.

Second, draw on state and local art councils, community arts and craft centers and school art departments. Contact them directly and ask for names and addresses of wholesalers who carry the materials you need. Summer camps and day care centers often have knowledge of suppliers and may be checked.

The third approach is word of mouth from other designers and craftspeople in your area. One of the major activities behind the scenes at craft fairs and art shows is the swapping of information among the exhibitors. If you see anything you like, ask!

And lastly, be sure to check the classified section of your telephone book, looking under every possible cross-reference, including trade associations. Stands to reason, wholesalers have telephones. But don't bother to call, unless you are looking for specific brand names. Just present yourself at their door and begin being charming.

Judy adds that a good time to present yourself to a new supplier is early in the morning, before he has really gotten into his regular business day. You will find he will spend more time with you and be more interested in hearing about your products. She strongly recommends keeping notes on your suppliers, and be as organized as you can during the shopping expeditions. Saves time and makes life easier for you and for them.

TRADE DIRECTORIES

There are two regional trade directories that might be helpful to you in pinpointing suppliers. A Blue Book

Market Guide covers the California market, including fabric, trimming and novelty wholesalers, notions and findings resources. Limited to the West Coast, it is available at modest cost from: California Fashion Publications, 1011 South Los Angeles Street, Los Angeles, California 90015.

The other, which I mentioned before, is Judy Glassman's *Craft Supplies of New York,* the second edition of which includes supplies in Connecticut, Long Island, New Jersey and southern New York State, in addition to resources located in New York City proper.

Judy is working on regional craft supply directories that will cover the rest of the United States, although these are not yet available. She is interested in rounding up as many good resources as possible and asks that anyone who has found a true treasure drop her a note with the name, business category and address so they can be followed up.

Letters and requests for *Craft Supplies of New York* go to: Workman Publishing Company, 231 East 51st Street, New York, New York 10022.

CONTINUITY

Continuity of materials is very important because you are showing your customers definite patterns and colors from which they are ordering. If you run out of the original color or shape or texture you cannot substitute without getting the buyer's permission. Counteract this danger by getting a clear understanding of the time limit that the goods you ordered will still be available for reorders from the wholesaler.

The time varies in different craft areas. Fabrics, outside of very basic types, have a relatively short continuity

period, while beads, buckles and jewelry findings sometimes continue for many months. Skins and hides, outside of basic shades, have a cut-off period as do most of
the materials that depend on season and fashion trends.
Feathers, however, are much less seasonal, with most
types available year-round.

When discussing continuity it is good to find out
whether or not the item you are buying is American-
made or an import, and if imported, from where. Dock
strikes, postal strikes, droughts and governments that
rise and fall are extra worries you simply do not need.

A funny story was told to me by a woman who once
designed place mats for a large plastic laminating company. She had done a fabulous line using reeds, beach
grasses and brightly colored butterflies, all encased in
clear plastic. The market response was great and the
orders rolled in.

The butterflies were imported from the Orient, however, and an unexpected rainy season wiped out the
supply. Without butterflies the place mats looked like
nothing, so she and her company spent a frantic two
weeks telephoning all over South America and Africa,
trying to reach lepidopterists who might have a backlog of pressed butterflies. The company was eventually
forced to cancel the line, but still gets an occasional note
from a butterfly collector from far away, asking if it is
still interested.

MINIMUM ORDERS

Once you locate a batch of good suppliers who will
deal with you, then you must check immediately on
what their minimum order requirements are. Minimum
order requirements tell you how little they will allow

you to order at one time. Sometimes this means how little you may order of one specific type of material, or one specific color or pattern—but sometimes it means how much total merchandise you must order at one sitting. Find out the specifics since it makes a big difference.

If you find the minimum orders are simply stupendous for the size of your business try to work out cooperative arrangements with other designers, hobbyists or craft centers where you group all your material orders under one name (usually whoever has the best credit rating) and then divvy up everybody's share after delivery. This is done all the time and is an effective way of cutting costs, even if it is applicable only to the most basic materials.

I did a lot of grouping when I first started out designing, thanks to a smart buyer at one of the local shops. She saw that my things were made of brightly colored fabrics rather similar in feeling to several other local designers. Very kindly she invited each of us to her shop, introduced us all, helped ease us through the initial suspicious, competitive moments, and then announced cheerfully that we could probably be of great help to each other.

We took her cue, began aiding each other, and grouped many fabric and trim orders. I often wondered if our buyers ever figured out that the same fabrics that were starring in sportswear were doubling in patchwork, pot holders, pillow covers, beach bags, and linings for anything that needed lining!

Which brings us to a point I want to make about material usage. In planning your line it is wise to aim for multiple uses of as many of your materials as you can. The most expensive supply is the one that can only be used on one certain item—perilous since that item might die an early death and you will be stuck with a backlog of the component parts that don't fit into anything else you are running.

For example, anyone producing garments eventually runs into needing hem binding that matches the garment color. We got around that by using narrow black or white lace edging instead of regular binding. We ordered lace edging in huge quantities, put it on everything, saved loads of money and were considered very chic and clever by buyers and customers alike who adored pretty lace instead of dull old matching rayon binding. We only had to stock black and white, which simplified our lives and our inventories, and the low price permitted us each to put lace on cuffs, necks and hems if we wanted, not to mention aprons, scarves and pillow covers.

Another possible way of saving on fabric is to sell off any sizable cutting scraps and leftovers to people making patchwork or appliqué. As a last resort, give away cutting scraps and leftovers to schools, community centers and hospitals. You will not recognize monetary gain but certainly will rack up points for getting into heaven by your good works.

MANFACTURING

PRODUCTION

As the chapter on costing indicated, the speed with which you make up your items is a vital part of the expenses and one which you should be constantly attempting to reduce. There are basically two ways to put a duplicative item together—in separate parts, or all at one time. The separate parts approach, sometimes referred to as "sectioning," consists of grouping all similar actions together and doing them as continuously as possible. Repetition speeds up any action and you will be able to cut down time and produce more if you can work it into your manufacturing process.

For example, if you are glueing a cut-out onto a bag, line up all your component parts and glue your whole week's production at one sitting. If you are sewing garments of similar colors, run up all the side seams in a row without stopping, and then clip the individual units apart after all the sewing is done. When Henry Ford first developed the assembly line techniques the world was awestruck. Use them; they still work.

The total unit approach is much less efficient, but necessary under certain circumstances. You can only throw one pot at a time on the potter's wheel. But you can group your production a bit and make a batch of similar shaped pots at the same sitting, and glaze them all at one time, etc. Industry has done many studies of the efficiency of factory workers and the results all point to repetition of hand motion as the key to rapid production. Sure, it's boring to do the same thing all day, but the faster you get through it the sooner you can move on to other activities.

SIZING AND GRADING

You can't be too careful about sizing and grading. If whatever you are making is supposed to fit something or somebody, you must be sure it really does. Unfortunately sizing and grading are complex skills that few nontechnical people are trained to do. Sizing is the manner in which each individual design is proportioned in order to fit the commonly accepted sizing standards in every field. Grading is the scaling up or scaling down of the original "sized" item so that an acceptable fit is achieved in many different sizes. Craftspeople and small designers have long been notorious for lack of fit and many buyers are wary of new lines that might bring them a flood of returns the day after purchase.

There are a couple of ways of handling the problem. You can, of course, study sizing and grading until you are able to do it yourself. Books keyed to the layperson are available in larger public libraries or from the book division of Fairchild Publications. Or you can hire somebody who is skilled in sizing and grading to go over your things whenever you make up a new line and set them up for you on a free-lance basis. This is not difficult to do unless you are in an area that offers you no manufacturing facilities.

Be careful about hiring the local tailor or dressmaker to size and grade for you. They basically work from the customer's body measurements and depend on custom fittings to make the garment comfortable. What you need is somebody experienced with paper patterns, who can take the one size you have done, and true it up to conform to all the normal sizes in your field, giving you back a set of paper patterns keyed for junior or misses, boys' or men's sizes.

Another alternative to the sizing problem is to use a pattern grading service in a nearby manufacturing area. Services are generally expensive but will get you through the problem until you are able to make other arrangements or can afford to hire a trained person to come and work with you several times a year. To locate a pattern-making service, check the yellow pages of the cities near to you, and check the classified ads in *Women's Wear Daily*.

A number of the larger New York City pattern services do a big mail order business with out-of-town designers who send them in a sketch or a sample garment and instructions on what they want to get back. Look through the New York City classified telephone directory if your local library has a copy, or write to whatever trade publication you read and ask the editor for a name or two. It's a lot of money and would have to be figured in your costing sheets but if it's the difference between things fitting and not fitting then it's worth it.

LABELING

Identifying your designs is something you'll have to face up to quite early in your business career. This is usually done with labels or stamps sewn into or printed on the underside of the piece—unless, of course, your name is so well known that it adds to the salability of the object. In the beginning, stick to the unseen areas that traditionally house identification. It is very important that your customers get to know your label and you begin to build up a following of loyal supporters who keep coming back for more.

When designing your personal label or imprint give some thought to how it will portray you and your business. You can appear whimsical, chic, innocent, hearty or any number of things just by your label, so be sure to pick out exactly what you want. Before you get down to placing an order even a rubber stamp, run through your favorite department store and read everybody else's label to get ideas on what the possibilities are.

Label manufacturers, of either woven or printed types, are listed in the yellow pages in larger cities, and in some of the trade publications. You may already be familiar with label companies from ordering children's summer camp labels from the consumer division of one of the larger manufacturers. It's smart to compare printed (less expensive) with woven (more expensive) labels for garments, and be sure to get data on minimums and delivery times for reorders. Be wary of self-sticking labels. They often are difficult to use on delicate materials and sometimes leave a sticky residue after removal.

I have found it is awfully easy to get carried away when designing and ordering labels. You may end up paying terrible amounts for some gorgeous thing that looks as if it were hand-done by Picasso. Restrain yourself and remember that each label costs you so much money on your Direct Material costing sheet. True, labels make a difference to the customer, but it's never the difference between buying and not buying.

If you are wholesaling to stores you might run into an anti-label attitude no matter how smashing your own label is. Many retailers, especially the larger stores who have built up a name and image for their business, are loath to have private labels used unless that label is so well known that it helps sell the merchandise. They want the customer to feel that their store has marvelous, unique items that are known only to them, and created especially for them. Which in many cases is almost true.

However, you as a designer want to get known around and build up a personal following, so both you and this type of retailer are working at cross purposes from the beginning. There is no good way of resolving this conflict, and since the retailer has the final say, even to the extent of cutting labels off merchandise as it is delivered, better just accept the injustice.

Sometimes you can turn it into a bit of an advantage by asking the buyer if your label would be welcome. If not, you save yourself the cost of the label and the time spent sewing it in. Some stores are aware of that and blithely send you their own label, expecting you to sew it in replacing your own identification. Just accept it.

Hang tags are another type of label that might be applicable to your designs. All the above data about labels also applies to hang tags—keep them simple and inexpensive, design them carefully, get printers out of the yellow pages, and expect that some stores will rip them right off as soon as they open up your boxes.

FEDERAL TRADE COMMISSION LABELS

If you are into apparel of any sort you run into a second type of label required by the United States Government. Back in 1914 an act of Congress established an agency named the Federal Trade Commission to keep tabs on how the business community was conforming to federal laws. On July 3, 1972, the F.T.C. passed a rule requiring care and maintenance instructions to be permanently affixed to all apparel.

This ruling is complex in that the manner in which a manufacturer furnishes the care and maintenance information is regulated. Other F.T.C. acts such as the Textile Fiber Products Identification Act and the Flammable Fabrics Act might also relate to your designs. To be on the safe side write to your local F.T.C. office and request free copies of all regulations pertinent to your field. Be specific in your note, stating exactly what materials you work with and in what market categories. The addresses for regional offices are listed in Appendix V, page 214.

PACKAGING

Depending on your product and your competitive market you might want to look into pre-packaging some of your work. This is really tricky for the novice to attempt and also can run into sizable amounts of money. Quick rule of thumb for wholesalers is to abandon all items that require pre-packaging and stick to a line that can be handled in bulk. If you are doing one-of-a-kind work, or retailing, you might find pre-packaging is right up your alley, and would solve some of the boxing and shipping of individual items.

Packaging, I'm sure you're aware, is really big business in the United States today. Awards are given out right and left each year for fabulous packaging designs and point of purchase display pieces. The manufacturer of boxes no longer just makes boxes, he now has a staff of creative advisers ready to dream up an image for your company and interpret the New You in glowing colors, smells, lights and sound. All of it costs a lot of money.

You will be told that distinctive packaging is the key to dollar sales, which is true in some markets but not in yours. Keep in mind you are filling a slot in the commercial market for unique hand-finished, low-volume products that are totally unattainable from the mass producers. Your things still retain the charm and honesty that personally produced work has, and that stamped-out-by-the-millions stuff has lost. Fancy packaging makes the mass-produced products look better. Yours already look good.

If you find some sort of packaging an absolute necessity, keep it as simple and as inexpensive as you can. Let your designs speak for themselves. And remember to figure the cost of the pre-packaging in on both your Direct Material and your Direct Labor costing sheets, in addition to the exterior packaging that you need in order to ship the bulk orders to your customers.

WORKERS

If you are building up a volume business, the day will inevitably come when you have to hire a worker or two. Hopefully, you have been looking ahead to this time and have a few people in mind. They might be neighborhood people or from a local craft center, art school or settlement house. Or they might be highly trained professionals who have worked in the trade for years, recommended by your suppliers, friendly competitors or from ads in the trade papers and magazines.

Step Number One is to check the laws covering workers and working conditions for your community. All three sets of government have their own requirements, so write or phone for the information booklets from the U. S. Department of Labor, Washington, D.C., your State Department of Labor at your state capital, and your local city or county labor office. They'll all have lots of literature telling you what is required of you and of your workshop or studio.

There are several arrangements for having people work for you. You can pay workers by the day or hour, or you can have them work by the piece or dozen, etc.

You can supply them with all the materials cut to size or pre-measured, or you can have them set up their own production. You'll have to select the arrangement that is most workable for you and the other person.

If you tend toward the hourly, daily or weekly wage you need to figure out some way of estimating in advance how much production you must get from your workers to make the whole thing feasible. An easy way is to make up a section of your production, timing yourself on every step so you can judge the number of minutes each action takes. Toss in whatever you instinctively know about your own speed—are you terribly slow or very fast—and come up with a figure that seems true. Do not expect miracles, so check it out on the basis that no two people work alike. You need to arrive at a general amount of finished items you can expect your worker to complete during each work period.

If you plan to hire pieceworkers you need the same timing data to let them judge whether or not they can be happy with your offering price. You will find you have done a lot of the timing while making up your costing figures, but take into consideration strange equipment, new patterns, etc. The best thing is to be very flexible with anyone working for you and really try to reason out a good arrangement with each individual, even though it might not be the same as you have set up with other workers. If everyone is pleased with the work arrangements, all of you will benefit.

Be sure you ask to see samples of the workers' craft, and let them examine samples of what you consider to be finished items. It saves a lot of agony if you establish mutual standards of acceptability before any time has been spent or products made up.

Once you and the craftsperson have agreed on a price you have to decide how the money is to be paid. Often small businesses are able to ease into being employers by using free-lance or part-time people in the beginning. As such, the craftsperson might be under the legal designation of "Independent Contractor" and not be considered staff that has to be covered by Workman's Compensation and Disability, plus Social Security and Withholding. Be sure to check with the Labor Departments of the federal, state and local governments—perhaps in the same letter asking for regulations on workers and working conditions.

Once you get a clear idea of the definitions of free-lance, part-time and independent contractor you can make a definite arrangement with your worker. Get the facts first and consider you have averted another potential disaster!

<h2 style="text-align:center">UNIONS</h2>

Usually when you first start out in business you will use non-union workers. As soon as you build up a large sales volume you will be expected to run a union shop. Theoretically, all workers should be represented by a union organization, but it is truly impractical to expect the local union representatives to bother with your studio if you are employing one or two part-time workers.

When you get big and become a factor in the local business community, affecting the economic welfare of a number of families, the union will want to represent your workers. Which is not all that bad, even though small-business people are innately wary of unions. By the time you are that size you will also be employing an accountant and most probably have some liaison with an attorney. Both of these specialists will be of great help to you when the question of unionization arises. Until then there is nothing you can do to prepare except to be sure the wages you are offering to your workers are within the legal wage levels, so your pricing structure will not be affected by a switch to a union shop.

An interesting side benefit of being acquainted with the local union representatives is that they often are a great source of advice. Since it is their business to keep track of all enterprises within their bailiwick, they know about you early on. And they know about everyone else in your area too, so if you need information about almost anything connected with your field, pick up the phone and ask them!

CONTRACTING

One of the most useful services the union offers you is to put you in touch with local contractors if you need large-scale aid in duplicating your designs. They know your area inside and out, and can put you in touch with contractors who have the exact equipment you need and who are accustomed to dealing in whatever quantity you require. Saves a lot of time and effort.

A contractor, by trade definition, is a business person who owns a factory full of equipment, and maintains a staff of skilled workers. In order to make his money he rents out the use of his equipment, operated by his own people, to designers and manufacturers.

The renting out is sometimes done by a time period like a week or two, or by a quantity unit, like a gross. The designer might supply all raw materials the contractor needs in order to make up the merchandise or he might simply pay the contractor to go out and purchase whatever is needed. If garments are being contracted, extra services like steam pressing may or may not be included. Packing and shipping are usually considered extras also.

The price for the work done is often settled jointly by you and the contractor going over your designs and fixing amounts of money per operation. In garment contracting, for example, so much money is charged for each button, buttonhole, zipper inset, side seam, pocket, etc. Sometimes the construction of the garment is simplified by the contractor who is, after all, the expert in putting things together.

A good contractor can make your life beautiful, and a bad contractor can be a disaster. Before you make any binding arrangements be sure to check recent references, and speak directly to other customers the contractor has done business with. And work out a mutually acceptable standard of finished work as you would with your own operators in order to avoid disappointments. Find out from the references how reliable the contractor is about meeting delivery deadlines so you can set a much shorter manufacturing time in order to be on time to your buyers.

Many myths circulate about dastardly contractors who take designs and knock them off, flooding the market with other people's pirated designs and not paying a penny. I'm sure some of this is true and just reinforces the need to check a number of references. True, he might give you all his relatives' phone numbers as his references, so hang in for a brand name label or a designer you've heard of before you sign a contract for work.

Another ugly rumor about contractors concerns stealing materials which are then claimed to be lost or damaged. Leather scraps, buttons, zippers and other parts that have some intrinsic value are most often reported as missing. If you have a suspicion about a contractor insist that he purchase the materials direct from you and you will buy back whatever usable leftovers are around when the finished products are delivered. This does wonders for keeping everything in proper order—especially with expensive raw materials such as furs, precious metals and skins. It also helps keep closer track of material utilization, resulting in less waste.

chapter IX

Seeing a Buyer

In due course of time, if you are wholesaling, you will have to actually go and see a buyer. Generally this is not without trauma.

Designer Gisella Heinemann, whose sportswear is enjoyed by women all over the country, has a marvelous way of describing it. Says Gisella, "My nose always runs when I see a buyer. And my slip shows and my stockings get runs in them. Occasionally a button falls off. I can find nothing in my handbag, and my pens go dry." Bear in mind this is a woman with a top reputation in her field. So if the thought of going to see a buyer turns you into jelly, understand you are not alone. Accept the fact that it will be difficult, but not impossible.

Everybody who wants to wholesale his things has to go see a buyer or two. And nobody feels comfortable doing it, even when you and the buyers are good, close, first-name-basis friends.

None of us enjoys being judged, being selected or rejected, and that's what happens every time you show your things to a buyer. The best you can hope for is that more items will be accepted than rejected. And the worst you can expect is that your work is so totally unacceptable that you should never darken the buyer's door again. Your reception will most probably fall someplace between these two extremes.

The amount of emotional involvement you still have invested in your products is generally the key to how much you are elated or destroyed by your buyer interviews. Keep pointing out to yourself that your crafts are strictly money-makers and not your children or your proof of your creativity. If the buyer says "no" she really means she thinks that the products you are showing her will not make money for her shop. Period. Nothing more.

If the buyer gets interested in your line and places an order it simply means that she feels the numbers she ordered will make money for her shop. Period. All this says nothing about your long-range success or failure as a designer/creator. The money-making potential of the few items you show the buyer is what is in question.

Another helpful thing to keep in mind is that the buyer will have to make the same decision every time you show her anything. The fact that you got stupendous orders from Buyer X last season doesn't mean a thing about what you can count on for this season. If your new crafts look like best sellers you'll get an order. If they don't, you won't get an order no matter how good your friendship is or how well your designs sold in the past.

Things can sometimes be changed a bit if you have

a lot of cooperative advertising money or promotion
plans to offer to the retailer who takes your line. But
as the beginning designer, all you have going for you
is the line you set out in front of the buyer, and your
orders will come or go on that alone.

MAKING THE APPOINTMENT

Adequate preparation for buyer visits helps a lot.
You can come across looking like a smooth professional
or a bumbling novice, depending on your preparation.
You have actually been preparing for the buyer visits
from the very beginning, when you first shopped at
the local stores to see which ones had merchandise
similar in feeling and price to yours; to see whose ideal
customer was also your ideal customer.

Given this information, you next need to narrow it
down to the name of the specific buyer, and telephone
to make an appointment. Don't bother to write. Buyers
are too busy to carry on a correspondence, especially
with an unknown designer. The accepted method is
a brief telephone conversation during which the buyer
or assistant buyer can swiftly figure out whether or not
your items sound interesting enough to give you an
appointment. But before you make the call, get yourself organized enough so you won't get turned down
on the phone. You've got to get enough solid information across in a minute or so in order to get the appointment.

There are certain specific points that will interest
the buyer. Make a list of them, rehearse a few times
and then make the call. The list should include:

Your name

A few choice words about what you do (your skill
   area)
A minute description of the products you want to
   show
A request for an appointment at the buyer's convenience

Sounds simple enough. So do it, and see how you
sound out loud. Define your skill area concretely. Say
"I am a hand knitter" or "I am a silversmith" rather
than "I have made up some things . . ." It helps the
buyer to visualize you and know whether or not there
is any point in seeing your things. If she is overstocked
on leather and you indicate that as your skill area she
might want you to call back at a later date. Be specific.

Be factual also about the line you plan to show the
buyer. "I would like to show you a group of pillows
with fabric appliqué covers" is better than "I have
done some really cute pillows . . ." Know what your
wholesale price range is for the entire line in case you
are asked. Sometimes large department stores have
budget and regular departments that carry similar
merchandise, with a cut-off point at a certain price
level. If you are asked to give some idea of your prices
it is probably to determine in which area you would
be selling.

An easy way to lead the brief conversation to the
point of setting up a visit is to ask what days of the
week the buyer normally sees new resources. Buyers
for large stores often have certain times set aside for
the reviewing of lines, and you will be told to come
then. The reserved times are often referred to as
"Buyer's Mornings" or hours. More about them later.

Most probably the assistant buyer will answer the
phone, and set up the appointment with you, or tell
you why you should not come over and show your

designs. Buyers are extremely busy people, and turn over lots of their routine work to assistants. Do not insist on speaking to the buyer personally. All you want is an appointment, which the assistant can easily set up. Buyers rarely return calls from unknown designers, I've found, so leaving your number is a waste of time.

At any rate, write down your facts and go over them in the privacy of your room until you feel somewhat easy about making the phone call. The rehearsal will save you from going completely blank when The Person is finally on the other end of the phone, or from chatting on and on and on from sheer terror.

Designer Joan Jablow tells a great story about her first phone call to the accessories buyer at Bloomingdale's. Joan had done an unusual group of belts and chokers, and all things pointed to Bloomingdale's as the store to contact first.

She finally pulled herself together and got the buyer on the phone. Being pretty verbal by nature, Joan felt herself slipping into a veritable barrage of words, telling the buyer more than anyone would ever want to know about the products, the market, Joan's family, and world in general. She had mental visions of the buyer sighing and holding the phone out at arm's length until she quieted down.

Finally Joan babbled to a halt. There was a long silence, and then the buyer said wearily, "Well, all right, come over ANYHOW."

TAGGING

After you have the appointment set up spend a little time getting your line ready for an easy presentation. Every item must be tagged with selling information for two reasons. First, having the complete data on each design written out and attached to the product insures that you won't forget or skip over any important information. You most probably will be nervous so the tag can act as a cue card in case you blank out!

Second, having all the information affixed to each item makes it easier for the buyer to get the whole story at one time if she wants to look more closely at it or wants to show it to somebody else in the store.

The usual way to handle tagging is to buy large, plain white paper hang tags at the stationery store, and then print or type the information on each tag. Get the kind of tags that come with a small string loop so you can safety-pin them on easily, or loop them through part of your product. For pottery, wood or other hard surfaces, tape the filled-out tag securely on the underside of the piece.

Include the following information:

1: *Style Number:* Make up a series of numbers for the items you plan to show, i.e., 100, 101, 102, etc., and tag each of the pieces in the order you plan to show them. Pick an absolute smasher for the first one of course, and then group them in whatever sequence makes sense to you. Above all, do not substitute cutesy names for the style numbers. You will feel pretty silly asking a deadpan buyer whether he prefers Purple Delight to Melancholy Baby.

2: *Sizes:* If the work you are showing has to fit anything or anybody, be very sure about your sizing. The first time I showed some tops to a buyer, claiming they were all size 10's, she whipped off her sweater, struggled into what was obviously no size 10, and gave me a terse lecture on the importance of accurate sizing as I was trying to peel the top back over her head. Be careful about pillow covers, too. It's embarrassing to stand there trying to stuff a standard pillow into something that suddenly seems to resemble an eyeglass case.

3:    *Colors:* Again, don't get carried away. If the products come in yellow and red, just say so, rather than announcing they can be ordered in Tropical Sunset and Tanager's Wing.

4:    *Special Care Factors:* Any special care factors or finishes that are important.

5:    *Prices:* List the price per item, per pair, by the dozen, the box, etc., wholesale only. Never tell a buyer what you think his retail selling price should be. That's his business.

6:    *Minimum order:* This relates back to your costing sheets and your production methods. Many items are unprofitable to make up one at a time. If your raw materials work out so that two or three is optimum and you don't think you'll be outpricing yourself, tell the buyer you have a minimum order of two or three per style. It's an accepted practice. But if you don't really have a minimum order, don't bother to dream one up.

7:    *Delivery time:* This is tricky in that it better be accurate or you are in trouble. Honesty is not only the best, but the only policy in quoting delivery times. Two to three weeks is the usual quote on small orders, but if it would really take you a full month to get a quantity together, say so. To insure your accuracy, go back over your costing sheets where you list how many you can make up in a week. Then if the buyer wants more than the quantity you figured, simply multiply it out, adding in any extra days you might need for purchase and delivery of additional raw materials. I have also felt that it is a good idea not to appear overeager. If you get a small initial order you might well be jubilant enough to assure the buyer she can have delivery in the next day or two. This is a mistake because it looks as if you have nothing else else to do, and sets a precedent for overnight delivery. Be cool.

8: *Terms:* Refer back to the chapter covering invoices. You probably won't tell the buyer your terms more than once during your presentation, but have it written on the tag in case he picks up something for a closer look.

CARRYING CASES

Once everything is properly tagged you have to figure out what you are going to carry it all in. New designers often knock themselves out thinking up fabulous ways to transport their things; making, borrowing or buying really out-of-sight containers to lug around the market. I've done it myself, and so has everybody else, but in the long run the carrying case makes no difference whatsoever as long as it works easily for you and appears to be neat and clean. Better a bright, fresh paper shopping bag than a slightly soiled leather tote.

The way the carrying case must work for you is so you can easily and rapidly take the products out, place them in front of the buyer, and then get them back into the case in split second timing. This takes a certain amount of practice, so rehearse a bit at home. You will probably wrap each individual item in tissue paper or in a plastic bag, so learn to handle those quickly and easily. You are going to have enough to

concentrate on without worrying about getting stuff in
and out of your bag.

SELLING POINTS

Make a brief list of what you feel are the selling
points of everything you plan to show the buyer.
Memorize them and practice delivering them convinc-
ingly. If the buyer is in a hurry you might not get a
chance to open your mouth, but have a few positive
facts at your fingertips just in case. These should be
slanted to make the buyer more interested in your designs and in you as a craftsperson.

For example, if you are showing pottery your selling
points might include:

1. The manner in which you worked on each piece,
   i.e., thrown on the wheel or hand built, or a
   combination of both.
2. Anything interesting about the clay, such as that
   you mix it all yourself; it is an unusual texture,
   color or perhaps it comes from a local area, or
   is imported from far away.
3. A word or two about the glazes you have used
   —are they under/over glazed, and how you happened to choose them.
4. Textures, if any—why you combined textures,
   what end result you were working for both
   visually and tactilely.
5. Multiple uses or groupings of your pots, if any.

And on your way to the interview don't forget to
tuck a pad and several pens into your carrying case,
handbag or pocket. It's amazing the number of designers who end up asking to borrow a pen and a piece
of paper in order to write down the order.

The actual presentation of your line will be simple and effective if you've done your homework. Usually the whole thing lasts only a few minutes—just enough to let the buyer get a quick look at what you've made. Small-store owner/buyers usually see you right out in a corner of the store, while department-store buyers will see you in their crowded little cubicle offices tucked back in odd corners of the floor their department is on. You'll be in, showing, and out again in jig time, emerging with an order, a turn-down, or perhaps a recommendation for you to see someone else within the store.

BUYER'S MORNINGS

"Buyer's mornings" or "buyer's hours" are slang expressions in the trade which refer to a way in which product lines are often reviewed by retail store buyers. Buyer's mornings are native to large, downtown department stores in major urban areas, and rarely occur anyplace else. They are set up to handle the largest flow of designers and salespeople in the shortest possible time and to free the buyer for other activities. As such, buyer's mornings are devastatingly impersonal and time-consuming to the new business person.

Here's how they work:

When the designers and salespeople come in they take numbers, like at the butcher shop or the bakery, and they wait until their number is called. The buyers sit in little cubicles behind the bottom half of a dutch door. The cubicles are spaced around the room, and it's quite medieval in appearance.

When your number is called you go up to the door indicated, show your things as fast as possible and then get your order or move on. No table or flat surface is available for you to spread your things out; it is all accomplished by what you can hold in your hands or balance on top of the narrow door. All in all, buyer's mornings are ghastly. No matter how little emotional investment you have in your products, you skulk home feeling misused, unseen and stripped of human dignity.

The reward, of course, is the order, and the unspoken understanding that once you've sold to a buyer and the transaction was satisfactory you will be invited to stop by her tiny office in the store and show your next line. No more buyer's mornings!

USE OF SLIDES

If your crafts are too large to carry all over town you have to devise an alternate way of showing the buyers your designs. The best alternate presentation method is the use of color slides and a small, battery-powered hand viewer. Take one or two actual samples of your work if at all possible, and let the slides speak for the rest of your line.

The slides themselves must be of good quality, designed to show the items as attractively as possible. Since the photos are not for reproduction you can take them yourself. Lighting is tremendously important. Use a solid color, light background, and photograph only one thing at a time. Bright sunlight usually works wonders, so go outdoors or on your apartment roof during warm weather. If you are showing garments it is a good idea to use some shapely friends as models, having them stand serenely in front of quiet backgrounds, using plenty of light. Don't try to emulate tricky fashion photography poses, just be simple.

Prepare your presentation carefully, labeling each

slide, and have all the tag data at hand. Rehearse the showing of the slides, and be sure the batteries in the hand viewer are new and bright. There are stories too numerous to mention about great presentations that were going superbly until the designer whisked the viewer into the buyer's outstretched hand only to find the batteries deader than a doornail. What can you say?

LEAVING SAMPLES

You might find that a buyer will ask you to leave your samples with him in order to show to some higher authority. A good rule of thumb is to turn this down in the friendliest way possible, since it is often a set-up used on novices to copy their items and cheat them out of a design fee or a legitimate order. Not always, mind you, because some buyers and stores are scrupulously honest. But the opportunity is there, and you'll never know until months later if you've been betrayed or not.

The way it usually works is that the buyer has an understanding with some of his closest suppliers, friends or contractors who have production equipment. If an item or a line comes in that looks good but is, perhaps, a bit high-priced, the dishonest buyer tries to borrow the samples, generally to keep overnight. If the designer leaves the samples they are quickly transported to the friend, copied or sketched, or even disassembled and then put together again so a pattern can be taken or a production diagram can be worked out.

The samples are then returned to the unknowing designer, along with the message that the items just didn't look right on second viewing, and thank you very much. Illegal, illicit, insulting and done all the time. Avoid this by offering to bring your samples back at another time.

A smoother version of this is practiced by some of the larger stores which have their own workrooms. Garments are the prey that is sought, usually novelty, and cut and sewn accessories. The buyer will place several small orders, until the consumer acceptance can be gauged. If the item sells out relatively fast, the garment is sent up to the retailer's own workroom to be produced there forevermore. And all you, the innocent designer, know is that the orders stop coming, and the buyer gives you no indication what went wrong. A month or two later your designs reappear on the shelves, minus your label, but done in similar basic materials.

There's no good way of combating the our-own-workroom gyp unless you decide to stop doing business with the store entirely.

"GETTING THE PAPER"

"Getting the Paper" is a quaint old expression used by the natives in the wholesaling trade to describe getting the official confirmation of an order from a retail buyer. If your line presentation is successful, the buyer will have you write up an order for some of your things. You will come to an understanding on the price and on the terms. You will go home happy, your order in your pocket.

Except if you are dealing with a sizable store. In which case the order in your pocket is merely a suggestion of an order, sort of a preliminary negotiation. In larger stores, with staffs of people and overlapping departments, the order is not considered official until you receive a confirmation back from the buyer, re-iterating everything that she wants to purchase.

The reasons for this are many, but the most basic one is that the buyer comes back from the market, having ordered many different items. The buyer's boss —the merchandise manager—gets everybody together every few days and goes over what each buyer has ordered, working toward an over-all picture of what will be in the store during a given time period. Then if your items are still in the fold you will be sent a confirmation signed by the buyer, actually ordering the merchandise. The confirmation will have an order number on it, and also a cut-off date. If the merchandise is not delivered before the cut-off date, properly labeled with the order number, it will be refused at the Receiving Room.

Word of advice: don't cut until you get the paper!

CONSIGNMENT

Consignment is another arrangement you will probably be asked to do quite early in the selling game. There are as many opinions on consignment as there are arrangements by which it happens. I personally do not like consignment and feel that it is unfair to designers. The usual consignment arrangement consists of some version of the following:

A designer places his work in a store. If the retailer sells it he pays the designer a pre-arranged sum of money. If the retailer does not sell the work the designer takes it back and gets nothing.

The advantage to the retailer is obvious. He can stock his store with new items at absolutely no cost or risk to himself. When stuff gets soiled and damaged he is under no responsibility to make good on it. And the disadvantage to the designer is just as blatant. The designer has already invested time and money. In the event the items don't sell, a lot of time is lost and the designer generally ends up with a batch of tired, shopworn samples that are no good for anything, not even gifts to one's friends.

The consignment game is favored among very small, very marginal shops that rarely have adequate capital to operate with. But the shop might well be chic and marvelous, absolutely the right place for your things. So your game plan must be to try to move the buyer off his "consignment only" position and into something that will work a little better for you. The retailer, on the other hand, is equally determined to stand pat, and will try to get you to believe that consignment is the only way of selling, and that you'll really miss out on everything unless you go the consignment route.

It's good for you to begin with a firm statement that you cannot do the usual type of consignment for some reason or other. I have found it effective to add that my accountant simply won't hear of it, thus lifting the onus neatly off me and onto some unknown being with the personality of Papa Bear. Whether or not you actually have an accountant is irrelevant.

Then try to make a deal that will be more beneficial to you. Suggest in view of the circumstances that the buyer make an outright purchase at your regular wholesale price of one of your designs, and you will add another two on consignment so there will be a nice group for the display case. Or try to make some arrangement where the buyer would pay you a deposit to be held by you that would cover replacement or repair in the event the crafts are stolen, or damaged and then returned.

It is hard to arrive at a blanket arrangement since each person you deal with will have different requirements, but try to avoid straight consignment at all costs. It brings you the least, at the most cost to yourself. And do not fall for the story that if you don't do consignment no one will ever handle your things. You might have to shop around a bit more, but retailers do exist who buy outright, and shun consignment. Their theory being, often, that anything they do not like enough to buy outright they do not like enough to have in their store. Good thinking!

SALES REPRESENTATIVES

Sales agents are always topics of great interest to small designers and craftspeople. Behind much of the interest is the feeling that perhaps one could hire a kindred soul to go out and do the dreaded buyer contact work, and thus avoid a very scary situation. Unfortunately it rarely works that way.

Sales agents, manufacturer's representatives, showrooms, outlets and jobbers do exist and their purpose is to do the selling for the actual creator. For this, and allied services, they collect a fee which is usually some percentage of the dollar volume they bring in. Sounds pretty good! And it is, but their income is totally dependent on how much merchandise they can turn over during any given time period; they are not too interested in bothering with a small, unknown designer who is not set up to produce volume. You normally have to have a proven sales record, guaranteeing them some judgeable amount of business, and therefore income, before they will talk business with you.

So cross them off your wishful-thinking list, and continue to do the selling yourself until you reach the point of being able to show an agent that he can figure on making X amount of dollars a month off your things. Then you might find that getting an agent or a rep is just what will make your life superb.

You usually find agents through the buyers you are already selling to. Your buyers will know the names of the people in the market who handle your type of item. They will also know who is reputable and who is not. Count on them for the best data when the time comes. Word of mouth is good also, so ask other designers you know, and check out your suppliers who just might be acquainted with the sellers of the trade.

Once you get away from personal recommendations it is riskier, but you can locate agents through trade papers, magazines, and even the classified section of the telephone book. In New York City you can contact the New York Association of Manufacturers Representatives at 1407 Broadway (212-354-7370) and ask for a number of names, but the Association referrals are set up to handle large volume. More about them later.

Once you locate a representative there are a number of arrangements you can make with the person. Whatever you work out, be sure to get it all down on paper, spelling out the individual responsibilities and details of all money and time transactions. Then get your banker friend, your accountant or a lawyer to check it over and interpret the fine print, just as you would with any business contract. Never just sign, in your eagerness for representation. Clarify the following:

1: Percentage of gross sales you will be charged as the representative's fee.

2: Manner in which percentages must be paid, and timing of payments.

3: How many samples, plus duplicates, they need, and at what times, for what duration.

4: Charges, if any, for display.

5: Charges, if any, for promotion, publicity, openings, mailers or catalog listings.

6: How you will be mentioned and credited in any written copy, and how much publicity you will get in relation to the other lines the agent is handling.

7: Who is responsible for checking the credit ratings of buyers.

8: Who is responsible if merchandise is not paid for, and the manner in which "no-pays" are handled.

9: Who is responsible for damage and theft while your samples are in the showroom or in the agent's possession.

10: Duration of the contract, provisions for releasing either of you from the contract, plus provisions for extending the contract.

11: Spell out that the contract only binds you for the specific kind of merchandise you originally offer to the agent, and you are free to work with other representatives on designs in non-conflicting areas.

12: Include, if possible, a gentle suggestion that you are under no obligation to make up design suggestions from the agent, or to copy best sellers from competitors unless you see fit. This sounds picky, but it can make your life miserable if it comes up regularly.

The New York Association of Manufacturers Representatives has drawn up a set of contract guidelines which will give you some idea how the larger manufacturers and representatives operate. The Association also has a standard application and resume form for designer/manufacturers who are looking for agents, showing the next step up the business ladder. A copy of these guidelines and a resume form can be found in Appendix VI, page 216.

SELLING SKETCHES AND DESIGNS

Another market for your skill could be selling your designs, patterns and/or sketches to manufacturers or publishers. This makes sense as an auxiliary effort to your own retailing or wholesaling, but is usually not enough of a money-maker to bother with alone.

At first glance it seems that all sorts of people buy designs and sketches. Fabric mills and print houses purchase pattern representations, yarn companies buy ideas for new uses, art needlework packagers buy styles to make up into kits, apparel and home furnishings manufacturers occasionally pick up a newcomer's ideas, and publications of all sorts buy items and instructions for their do-it-yourself pages.

Unfortunately the competition is unbelievable, the pay is wretchedly low and the chances of your designs being stolen and copied are very good if you deal with anything but the top level companies in your field. So be forewarned!

To approach design selling you must make up a portfolio of your sketches, paintings or actual items, complete with instructions for making up duplicates, if you are showing non-artwork samples. The portfolio should include at least a dozen pieces of artwork, or four to six

actual craft items. Don't bother to mat and frame paintings and sketches. Just have them neatly done on rather
large art paper. If you are showing knitted, crocheted or
sewn crafts have the make-up instructions typewritten,
specifying the size of yarn, needles, stitches per inch, and
size of finished sample garment.

Use the local yellow pages to help you pinpoint manufacturers who might be interested, plus the library and
the trade publications you read. Make up a list of prospects and begin telephoning each company, asking if
they buy designs from outside people, and if so, when
you could come and show your things. As with any "asking" phone call, rehearse it first so you won't forget
anything.

If you find no local organizations that might be buying designs you can work out a letter and send it to companies in nearby manufacturing areas that you could
possibly visit if necessary.

Alas, after all this work, the prices that you can expect
to be paid are minimal. The going rate in the larger
manufacturing cities for apparel designs or sketches is
between $10 and $15 per sketch from a new designer.
Fabric patterns and prints are rarely ever purchased from
novices who have little technical knowledge about the
big power machinery used to create or reproduce the pattern. The few purchases I know of have been under $50,
and the designers haven't been exactly unknown.

Yarn companies are slightly better prospects for the
newcomer. Companies that publish their own pattern
books showing how to knit, crochet, hook or stitch their
yarns into great new items generally have a good-sized
staff, working under a knowledgeable fashion director.
Still, if an unknown designer has an absolutely outstanding item it might be purchased by a company. The

going rate, however, for the finished product plus clear, complete make-up instructions runs as low as $50, and seldom rises above $250, including directions for making up many sizes rather than just the one in which the item was originally made.

A better bet, almost, would be to work out a few of your really outstanding designs, grade them up into several larger and smaller sizes, reprint them yourself and try to sell them as a complete package to local yarn and fabric shops in your city and in neighboring towns.

All in all, selling designs and sketches is one of the most difficult ways to earn money using your craft skill.

chapter X

Publicity and Promotion

Publicity and promotion are often ignored by the new business person simply because there are only so many hours in each day. Better to get the work turned out, the phone calls made and the bills typed up. However, it's a mistake to view publicity as a luxury that can wait until that wonderful day When There Is Time.

Publicity on various levels is a necessity for the business person no matter how tiny the business enterprise is. Approach publicity as a way to make your selling job easier, as a way to open doors for you, and then you will see it in a different perspective. You can do without luxuries but the necessities must be tended to regularly.

PERSONAL PUBLICITY

Your first concern is personal publicity. This is the publicity that tells your neighbor and your local retail

144

store buyer that you are a talented designer producing a certain type of item. Everyone has read or heard interviews with creative local personalities on radio, television or in newspapers and magazines. The article or broadcast generally begins with a brief introduction of the person, telling what she is doing, how she manages to do it, and why she is doing it. We are all interested in hearing about other people's lives and work. It is time to begin telling other people about your life and work.

This brings us face to face with the built-in reluctance of many creative people to toot their own horn. How much better to be "discovered" by the public than to push your way into people's awareness. The movie-starlet-discovered-at-the-soda-fountain is a myth we all adore. But such discoveries don't happen often enough to be practical. More movie stars have been created through diligent effort than by idle chance.

Unattractive as it seems, you'll just have to make up your mind to publicize yourself. Be your own best product. Eventually, when you become established, known as That Talented Designer, you can hire a professional publicist if you desire. Until you get some sort of a "name" you have to do it yourself.

And it's not so impossible to do. From where you sit, in your studio or workroom, the newspaper, magazine, radio and television people look very distant and forbidding. But from inside the editorial room or the broadcasting studio things look different. A certain amount of space or time must be filled up each day or each week or each month with information that the world in general will find interesting.

A relatively small portion of your daily newspaper is devoted to the latest news. Most of the space is concerned with non-current events coverage. The editors and broadcasters have to find good information to fill up all that non-news space and time. Which is where you come in.

You are doing something interesting. You are designing and producing handcraft items that are for sale to the public. You are different from your next-door neighbor. And you are different from other hobbyists you know. You are in business to make money, albeit in a modest way. You have gotten it all together, perhaps in your spare time, perhaps in your home, usually in a noncommercial work situation.

You have figured out how to juggle your time and personal life to make room for your business. You have learned to create and produce items that are good enough to be considered commercial. You have dug up suppliers who will deal with your small volume needs. You know how to cost your products and how to present them to a customer.

Actually, you have done an awful lot. You are an interesting person. And therefore of interest to editors and broadcasters in your area. Not the cover of *Time* or *Newsweek,* not yet, but you are of definite interest to local newspeople. Never underestimate the word "local" in your publicity efforts. We are all fascinated by what is going on in our community.

William Randolph Hearst, legendary newspaper baron, was reputed to have made the classic "local" statement when in Chicago he said, "A dogfight on Rush Street is worth two wars in the Balkans." Be the dogfight on Rush Street.

Your first step is to research the local press and the broadcast media to see what outlets are available for personal publicity on Fascinating You. Read everything

daily, weekly or monthly put out anywhere near you, including newsletters, community group bulletins, etc.
And listen and watch all local radio and television broad-
casts that might carry interviews or mentions of local
people who do interesting things.

Make a list of all the programs or print media that
might be worth contacting. Get specific. Include names,
addresses, telephone numbers and zip codes. This is the
beginning of your personal press list. Given a proper
amount of tender loving care, this press list will grow
and flourish, bringing you pleasure, fame and perhaps
even some new friends.

WRITING A "BIO"

Then write a one-page description of you and your
business. Your one page doesn't have to win an award
for creative writing but it must be concise, clear and
present the facts in an interesting manner. A quick way
of organizing the data is to make the following list on
a piece of scrap paper:

WHO
WHAT
WHY
WHEN
WHERE
HOW

Then just fill in the facts. Who: You—with a tidbit
or two to make it interesting . . . you, a graduate of art
school, and hobbyist sculptor, have now opened a business making ceramic wall hangings . . . or perhaps you,
mother of seven, having always made your own children's
clothing, are now offering a group of your own designs

. . . etc. And be sure to include specifics on how or where the reader can buy your products.

Get the information down on paper and you'll be surprised how interesting it is. Without going into vast detail let your reader know how you happened to be making and selling things. Generally there is a pretty good story behind the beginning of every business. Including yours. Type up a clean copy of your one-page story and you are ready to contact the most logical person on your press list.

CONTACTING THE PRESS

Many craftspeople find the contact work troublesome, and for some it truly is. Relatively few of us can breeze in, set something up with an editor we've never met before, and then be on our merry way with nary a gulp or a shiver. Don't worry if you get your press list made up, your one-page biography typed, and then find yourself paralyzed.

A very talented leathercraftsman I know once told me each season when the time comes for him to call the editors he begins to have a recurring nightmare. In the dream he picks up the phone, gets the editor on the line, says this is Joe Smith, and the editor responds with "So what?" End of dream. Cringe.

Chances are it's not going to be easy, but there are two approaches to choose from. The first way, which I know works best for me, is to write the editor or broadcaster a one-paragraph letter on my business stationery telling him I am a listener/reader of his, doing something I think his audience would find interesting, and I am enclosing a one-page summary of my work. At the end I say I would like to talk with him and will telephone

his office next Something day in the middle of the afternoon to see if we could get together.

Then I wait until the day and time I mentioned in
the letter, make the phone call, and usually have been
able to make an appointment. Or else I am told why
my story is not of interest to him at that time. If an
editor or broadcaster tells me he has a big backlog of
material and is not taking anything new at the moment
I ask when would be a good time to re-contact him. And
I mark my calendar and follow through with a phone
call at the time he has suggested.

The other approach is to call direct, without a letter.
Be ready to give all the facts on the telephone, ending
up with the offer to mail your one-page summary to
him, or to stop by and meet him at his convenience. If
you feel you can handle the direct phone call without
sounding like an idiot, do it. It will save you a lot of
time and effort and you will know if the editor or broadcaster is interested in you immediately. If he says no,
find out why. Then just dial the next number on your
press list and keep on going till you have something
definite set up.

Then stop for a while. Nothing gets an editor angrier
than finding out too late that the person he has just
interviewed has also gone to every other paper in town
with the same story. If you get a commitment from one
paper, station or magazine, a good rule of thumb is to
wait at least a month after publication before you try
to set something else up with a competitive station. You
are not putting all your eggs in one basket when you
wait, you are merely being professional and recognizing
that each editor is trying to bring special feature material to his readers that will not be duplicated all over
town.

PHOTOGRAPHS

Sometimes an editor will ask you if you can furnish a photograph that can be used in the write-up. Be honest and if you really can't come up with a professional quality picture, say so. A clear, well-lighted black and white 8" x 10" glossy print is what is needed. No polaroid shots, or color slides or prints. Check out the kind of pictures your editor has used on other stories. If you can take one, or have a photographer friend who can, then agree to supply photos. They really make a story more interesting. But beware of misleading an editor. If you welch out on pictures he is expecting, he has every right to be annoyed.

Larger papers will sometimes send a staff photographer out to take his own pictures. If this happens be sure to ask the photographer how you would go about getting prints made of his photographs in case you want to send some out yourself. Negatives are usually kept on file a short time after the photograph is used. Check prices of prints and delivery times.

PROMOTION: THE SECOND STEP

Once you get a write-up anyplace then you can begin to do some promotion work for yourself, too. The publicity is when the press tells the world in general about you and your products. The promotion is when you use copies or reprints of that write-up to tell specific people about your business and yourself. This is also referred to as "re-merchandising" your product. Whatever you call it, it is a smart thing to do.

As soon as you are written up anyplace get several copies of the publication. Cut out your article, including photos if any, and cut the name of the publication and publication date from the top of the first page. Glue the article, name, and date down on a sheet of plain white paper, and have it duplicated to be used as a mailing piece. Sometimes home or office copy machines will give you a clear reproduction. If not check your local phone book for the nearest printer who does "off-set" work, or photocopy printing. This is a quick and inexpensive way to duplicate printed material.

For a few dollars you can have a hundred copies made of your press write-ups and you can begin mailing them out to everyone you want to see the article. You may decide to send copies to stores you plan to contact in the near future—paving the way for your letter or phone call. You certainly will want to send copies to everyone who has bought from you in the past.

I always found it beneficial to send copies of my press write-ups to the wholesalers I was buying my supplies from. When I first started my business I was buying in such small quantities that the wholesalers and jobbers were quick to complain that my business was more bother than it was worth. I felt that by sending them copies of my press write-ups I was showing them I was getting rich and famous and soon would be ordering larger quantities of everything!

When you are getting your write-up, publication name and date ready to take to the photocopiers it is sometimes helpful to glue the pieces down in such a way that you can use the sheet as notepaper too. Not for long letters, but if you need to drop a note or write a line or two, you will have room to do so.

Once you get several press write-ups, then you can do a larger promotion piece, glueing the individual articles, names and dates all on one large piece of paper, overlapping them so they look good. With this you can really dazzle all comers, showing you are well known and well regarded in your field. Once you get to the stage of doing a large mailing piece it is wise to have more than one hundred printed up. Use the large mailer as an envelope stuffer in everything you send out for a month or so. And do a mailing to customers you haven't contacted yet. Put copies up on local bulletin boards, including easy directions on how the reader can go about purchasing your items. (Libraries and laundromats are good for this.) Every little bit helps!

TRADE PUBLICITY

If your business goal is more sizable than just local selling you will want to begin doing publicity for your items in the trade papers and magazines. Conversely, if you are not interested in building up a bigger business, skip the trade press. Publicity you place in the trade press will be read by retailers across the country, and by other designers, manufacturers and publications people. It is much harder to get written up in the trade press, but not totally impossible. Trade publicity can take either the form of your own personal publicity or can publicize your line rather than yourself.

If you decide you want to be written up as that talented designer who started from scratch, then use the same technique and one-page story that you would use to contact the editors and broadcasters in your area. First research the trade press to decide who and where you should make your contacts. Make up your personal trade press list, with names, telephone numbers and addresses. Either write an introductory letter with your one-page story enclosed, or make the telephone call if you are in the same city as the publication staff.

Chances are the trade press will not be located in the same area you are in so be prepared to carry on the contact work by mail. If you send off your letter and story and do not get any response, send a duplicate a few weeks later. The important thing is to be sure your research is correct, and you are sending the data to the staff person who could use the story. Never send anything to a publication unless you have a person's name to direct it to.

Competition for write-ups in all trade papers is much more intense than in your local newspaper and magazines. Every manufacturer and designer wants publicity, and most larger organizations have professional P.R. people who do nothing but publicity and promotion all day. Your chances of breaking into print in *Women's Wear Daily* with a personal story on Talented You are pretty slim unless your personal story is incredibly unique. However, as you will see by your constant reading of the papers, unknown designers do get written up occasionally, so it's worth a try. But don't take it personally if you are turned down. The odds are against you to begin with.

The chances are slightly better for you to place some publicity on your products. One of the main purposes of all trade publications is to keep the readership informed of new products, new styling, new organizations and new designs. Each time anyone important brings out a line the opening is covered by the trade press. Reporters or editors see the new products and write them up for the publication. Buyers read the publication each day and keep notes on what sounds right for their store, what they will check into next time they go to market.

The trade press must cover all the established manufacturers and name designers. After that, if space is left in the paper, unknown lines that are exciting and unusual will be written up. Unfortunately, everybody has to bring his line out at the same time, which makes the competition even tougher.

The initial research is best done on your own line, rather than going to the library to check out whom you should be contacting and where. The key words are "exciting and unusual" and you must go through your products and attempt to evaluate whether or not anything you've got is outstanding enough to be really newsworthy.

I found it helpful to ask the handful of buyers I felt were friendliest and closest to me whether or not I should go to all the trouble of making up a publicity release or doing a mailing on a given item. Everybody knows publicity is costly and time-consuming so the answers were usually honest. If the answers were enthusiastic yesses then it seemed worth the extra work. But if the answers were lukewarm I would skip it.

These same buyers might be placing good volume orders and enjoying brisk business on my things but what I needed to know was not whether or not the buyers liked them. I needed feedback on whether or not one specific design was exciting and unusual enough to be newsworthy in the trade. A totally different story.

MAKING UP A PRODUCT
PRESS RELEASE

If you have an item that passes the "exciting and unusual" test then it makes sense to send out some publicity on it. The press release takes a very specific form, consisting of a black and white 8″ x 10″ glossy photograph showing the item clearly and attractively, plus a write-up of the important selling points describing the product.

Again, if you cannot take an acceptable photograph yourself get a professional or a very knowledgeable hobbyist friend to do it for you. A few designers I know have had great good luck taking brightly lighted black and white shots with a Kodak Instamatic and then getting glossy blow-ups made. More designers I know, including myself, have had dismal failures taking their own press pictures. Suit yourself, but make sure, no matter who does the photography, your items are clearly visible and attractively shown.

The information sheet should be a full sheet of standard typewriter paper. This is necessary since you will glue the data sheet to the underneath lower edge of the photograph so it can be folded up over the picture to form a protective cover, guarding the photograph from scratches and surface damage.

The professional press release is quite standard in structure, beginning with a sentence or two of descriptive copy giving the selling points of the item. For example, a fall release on a teen-ager's leather bag might start out with a few lines about "Smart girls get A's in fashion when they go back to school with a roomy pouch bag of kangaroo leather . . ." A spring press release on beach hats might begin with some copy about the summer sun never scorching the sophisticated mermaid who wears, etc.

After the introduction skip a few spaces and list the selling facts:

STYLE NUMBER
SIZES (IF ANY)
COLORS

FABRIC OR MATERIAL INFORMATION
AVAILABILITY
OTHER PERTINENT DATA

Finish off with the phrase, "For further information contact Ms. XX," plus your company name, address and phone. Be sure to include zip code and area code numbers. You might want to put "For immediate release" or for release after whatever date suits you if you want to time your mailing in some way.

Glue the press release page to the underside of the lower edge of the photograph, mail flat in a large enough envelope so the photograph will not be bent or damaged, and always use a cardboard stiffener. Never write on the envelope after you have inserted the photo since pen markings can go right through and damage the surface of the picture, undoing all your good work before the editor even gets to open his mail!

As I said before, the competition is very tough and huge quantities of professional press releases and photographs flood every editor's desk every day. Because of the quantity received, photographs and releases are never returned. But if you feel that your things qualify and if you have the extra time and money, begin to send out trade publicity. A write-up in the trade press is a gigantic step forward for a new designer, and the re-merchandising promotion is mandatory.

RE-MERCHANDISING TRADE PUBLICITY

As soon as you get your copies of your write-up, paste the whole thing up and have it duplicated. Spend some time in your local library going through the consumer publications your customer reads, making a list of stores credited in the magazines that are in other parts of the country but carry merchandise similar in feeling to yours. This data is usually found in a "Where to Buy It" section somewhere near the back of the book.

Get a list of such stores together and mail out your trade press write-up reprints along with a letter addressed to the attention of the buyer of the department you wish to sell to. In the letter say you feel your products would be of interest to the buyer, draw attention to the reprint from the trade paper, and offer to send samples or fabric and material swatches or additional photographs if you have them. In this way you use the publicity in an attempt to actually extend your business.

Use trade press reprints as mailers to old and new customers and to suppliers. Since few trade publications are known in the consumer world you can skip the local bulletin boards.

SHOPPING COLUMNS

Shopping columns appear in most of the consumer magazines, and sometimes offer a potential consumer publicity outlet to the new designer. These columns are generally placed toward the back of the magazine, after the bulk of the editorial pages. They show tiny photographs of products, plus brief write-ups of the item, including information on how they can be purchased by mail. Competition to be included in shopping columns is fierce since the magazines are nationwide, and acceptances are rare.

The major home furnishings magazines, sadly enough, pursue a policy in their shopping columns of showing only products that are also being advertised in the magazine. Advertising is prohibitively expensive for the beginner craftsperson so the ad-only rule effectively bars any exposure you might get if your products were included in the shopping columns.

National fashion magazines have a much less restrictive policy and do accept a certain number of products every month for inclusion in the shopping columns. Use the same approach and material you would send out for trade publicity. Send a photo and the accompanying press sheet direct to the attention of the shopping column editor, whose name you will get from the masthead of the magazine. Be sure to include all selling information plus clear directions on how the reader can purchase your products.

CREDITING

You might want to give a "credit" to a few of your favorite retail stores that do mail order business so the reader can write away to the store to order your product. Always check the store buyer first for permission to list them on a press release since some stores have strict policies about publicity. This sort of offer usually endears you to the buyer even if the store says it cannot accept the credit!

If you don't want to credit a store, have an address the reader can send to, enclosing a check or money order and you will mail back the product. Be aware, though, that if the item does get into the shopping column it might suddenly become a smashing success and you will be saddled with wrapping and mailing every individual order, along with the rest of your work. Also, if you are going to list your own name and address be sure to look into the sales tax laws in your state covering direct mail.

A last word on publicity and promotion. Not only is

it professional protocol but also human good manners to send a short thank-you note or telephone call to any editor or broadcaster who has used your material. Never goof up on this. Do it regularly and each time you re-contact that person your chances of being remembered favorably increase. Whether we like it or not, people tend to do more for friends than for strangers.

chapter XI

Craft Fairs and Outdoor Art Shows

An additional way of selling crafts that is fun, exciting and reasonably profitable is through local craft fairs and art shows. These events are major marketing activities for some craftspeople who are wary of the wholesale/retail pressures, but fairs can also be utilized as a pleasant addition to your regular selling channels. No end of products qualify for inclusion in a craft fair. From apparel to *objets d'art*—they all make the scene—and perhaps you should too!

Permit me to dazzle you with a few statistics gleaned from the excellent material available from the Interagency Craft Committee, Farmer Cooperative Service, United States Department of Agriculture, Washington, D.C. According to the Committee, marketing prospects for craft fairs are good, and getting better. For example, the Southern Highland Handicraft Guild in Asheville,

North Carolina, sponsors two craft fairs each year, and tracks the sales figures as follows:

Year	Sales at Fairs
1965	$ 76,110
1966	$ 89,470
1967	$110,122
1968	$136,084
1969	$159,006

Sales figures for subsequent years are unavailable, but the rate of increase holds true, I understand.

The West Virginia Department of Commerce released the following figures showing the remarkable growth of the annual Mountain State Art and Craft Fair held near Ripley, West Virginia:

Year	Craft Sales	Attendance
1963	$ 7,500	6,576
1967	$25,700	20,199
1969	$70,000	42,000
1970	$91,064	45,000

The Kentucky Guild of Artists and Craftsmen published the following figures on their annual outdoor craft fair at Berea College Forests:

Year	Craft Sales	Attendance
1967	$ 8,317	5,000
1968	$12,779	7,500
1969	$18,718	7,411 (bad rains)
1970	$35,988	12,252

In another Department of Commerce publication dated January, 1973, Donald L. Page, executive secretary-treasurer of the West Virginia Artists and Craftsmen's Guild, estimates that "the combined incomes of some 2,000 participating craftsmen in the West Virginia fairs alone could approach as much as $2 million annually."

The statistics are similar in other parts of the United States, so I won't elaborate. Let it suffice to say that the market certainly is there, and perhaps you should be, too.

Craft fairs have no hard and fast structure. They vary from the gigantic operations cited above to something that resembles the church bazaar or school fund raiser. They can be organized by professionals, aided by local, state or federal staffs and money, by regional or local craft leagues, or simply by a group of people who get together to put on a show.

They can be held indoors or out, have an admission charge for the public or let everybody in for free, be a spin-off of another event such as a state or county fair, be expensive to show in, be inexpensive, be restricted as to exhibitors or open to every person who wants in.

As such, it is difficult to generalize about craft fairs. However, a few explanations and descriptions might be helpful to you. The first is the difference between an open show and a juried show.

OPEN SHOW OR JURIED SHOW

As it sounds, an open show is one in which any craftsperson is welcome to come and participate, exhibit space permitting.

A juried show is one where a jury of expert gallery, museum staff, or local authorities sets up a screening panel which passes on the acceptability of every would-be exhibitor's work. The famous Washington Square Outdoor Art Show in New York's picturesque Greenwich Village is typical of a juried show.

Leif Wicklund, potter, and partner in Sexwick Pottery of New York, is one of the jury members for the crafts section of this show. In judging the pottery entries he looks for some of the following points:

1: *Competence*—command over the materials; technical competence shown by proper execution of each sample'piece.

2: *Understanding of the craft*—for this Leif views the samples (minimum of three) as a group which indicates where the potter is in his field. This also rules out hobbyists who cannot consistently turn out quality work.

3: *Innovation*—what the designer is attempting to say in his work that is different from other craftspersons. This criterion helps rule out copies of trendy work that is already on the market, or work that is representative of a certain teacher or school of pottery. In order to become a full-fledged craftsperson, Leif feels that the individual must absorb the instruction he has received, integrate it into himself, and then "take off" on his own, creating works that are uniquely his. Innovation is an important category since it establishes the would-be exhibitor as a master of his craft or as a student still developing his design force.

Please understand that these categories are not necessarily used by other juries screening for other shows. They are merely the guidelines used by one person. I include them here because they help underline some of the differences between merchandise that would be acceptable in craft fair selling rather than merchandise that would be designed to show to a retail store buyer. It's a tricky definition lying somewhere between duplicative, trend-reflecting pieces for the retailer, and one-of-a-kind works that the gallery owner would be shown.

For craft fair selling you need not make up a dozen or so identical copies of one design, although you can make up a dozen or so interpretations of one theme. And the buyer, be she consumer or retailer, knows that the craft fair is not the place to shop for sets of matching mugs, plates, pillows, etc. If everything must be identical, the buyer goes to the mass producers whose standardized production methods guarantee no variation between items. Much of the charm of the craft fair merchandise is the uniqueness of each piece.

TIMING

The timing of the craft fairs varies in different parts of the country. Many, of course, are planned for summer months so they can be held outdoors or in conjunction with state and county fairs. November is another great craft fair month, taking advantage of the Christmas and holiday gift-buying needs.

Some craft fairs are held as fund raisers for non-craft organizations, scheduled to meet a budget deadline that falls at the ending or beginning of a fiscal year. Schools and craft centers often hold their fairs in June marking the end of the school year, clearing away to close down for the summer.

The duration of the craft fair varies from a week or ten days down to one afternoon or evening. Weekends during the summer are often selected for fairs held in or near resort areas.

FEES

Pleasantly enough, the fees to participate in craft fairs are quite modest, seldom getting above $50 in any part of the United States, and generally hovering between $10 and $25. The entry fee is normally paid when you register for the show, and in the case of a juried show, when you are notified that your work has been accepted by the jury.

The entry fee buys you a number of delights, depending on the set-up of the fair. Primarily it buys you your exhibit space, the square footage assigned to you in which to exhibit your work. Occasionally this exhibit space comes equipped with a table and chair, but most often it is merely an area marked off on the grass or on the floor. What furnishings you need must be provided by you.

On shows that extend overnight or several days, the entry fee generally covers the services of the security guards hired by the fair entrepreneurs so you need not pack and store everything you brought each night. For outdoor shows you must provide your own weather security, and are solely responsible for covering and protecting your pieces from dew, rain, or excessive sunlight.

Some shows have printed catalogs or programs crediting and describing each exhibit. The entry fee usually covers inclusion in the catalog except when the fair is set up from inception to be a cooperative effort, and everyone is expected to kick in for the production of the program.

A final goody your entry fee sometimes brings on long shows is a list of available accommodations, campgrounds, local stores and restaurants. Rarely does a fair offer accommodations outright, but if dormitory space is available nearby, an arrangement is often set up to offer housing to the exhibitors at minimal cost.

The entry fee also brings you the assurance that the fair operators will provide you and every other exhibitor a goodly amount of publicity, posters, handbills and other promotion to attract crowds of customers. This sometimes gets sticky, though, since the standards of how much promotion is enough promotion vary widely between operators and exhibitors.

In lieu of an entry fee, some craft fairs take a percentage of the gross receipts made by each exhibitor. The range currently seems to be between 15 percent and 30 percent. The responsibility of reporting accurate sales figures usually rests on the craftsperson. All the other arrangements are similar to those of an entry fee show.

WHOLESALE DAYS

A growing trend, and one I heartily endorse, is the establishing of "wholesale days" at some of the larger craft fairs. Attendance for the first day or so is restricted to credentialed retailers who are invited to attend by the show's management. After the buyers have shopped and placed orders for later delivery, the doors are opened to the general public who can purchase the individual pieces and take them along home.

Potter Bob Sedestrom of New Paltz, New York, had a wonderful encounter with a retailer at one of the very first attempts to have a wholesale day at a fair. Credentials were checked and re-checked, wholesale terms worked out, much business vocabulary was rehearsed by the craftspeople, and finally the big day arrived. Everyone was unsure of the ground rules.

A buyer approached Bob, liked his work, wanted to place an order, but seemed quite troubled. Finally the man confessed that he had no local credit rating. and had forgotten his checkbook. Would it be all right with everybody if he just paid cash was the hesitant request!

Even if no fair time is set aside exclusively for retailers, some local shop owners are bound to show up,
so be sure you have figured out in advance your whole-
sales prices, minimum orders, terms and delivery dates.

PROMOTION

You can do as little or as much promotion for yourself during the fair as you choose. A "must" is business cards, placed prominently in your display area. A
close second in importance if you are serious about
building up loyal customers is to use the fair to compile
a mailing list. Since you are selling direct to the consumer, your sales are considered to be at the retail
level; you must charge sales tax, issue a receipt to the
customer and keep a carbon copy for your own records.
Make sure you include the customer's full name and
address on the receipt. Stash your carbons away in a
safe place during the fair, and work out a mailing list
at home at your leisure. A simple, one-page mailing
piece with photos or sketches, descriptions and prices
of new items you have made up should be sent out
every six months or so to the mailing list. Be sure to
include how-to-order instructions, with a "tear-off at
the dotted line" section to be sent back to you along
with a check or money order. Much more about this
type of selling in Chapter XII, which covers mail order.

DISPLAYS

The importance of your display cannot be over-
emphasized. As retailers have known for centuries, an
attractive presentation of merchandise often makes the
difference between sale and no sale. Since it is so crucial,
begin planning out your showcase as soon as you get
the dimensions of your exhibit space, and data on

whether or not a table and chair are furnished by the operators. Keep your method of transportation in mind so you don't end up dragging cumbersome furniture over hill and down dale.

A good way to approach creating your display is to check out how local shops handle display counters, shelves, tables, baskets, etc. Any tips you can glean from the pros are fine! Then do a few sketches relating to the size and shape of your exhibit space, and see what sort of presentation pleases you and is in keeping with the feeling of your crafts. Work toward simplifying each sketch, crossing out as many extraneous details as possible. Keep your budget in mind. No sense in blowing your potential profit re-creating the Gardens at Versailles.

Use crisp, clean-looking display units that can be kept in good condition with a minimum of effort and are easy to transport and assemble. Painted pieces of pegboard or plywood that bolt together into interesting shapes are good, as are pieces of clear lucite placed on blocks of wood or bricks. If you want any sort of banner or sign over your display area be sure to figure out in advance how to hang it up or attach it to your table. Keep playing with your display ideas until you come up with something that can be prepared at home, is economical, functional, and looks as if you designed it.

DRESSING ROOMS

If you are planning to sell some type of clothing try to make provision for a try-on booth. The number of sales skyrockets when customers can check out the fit before they purchase. An easy dressing room area can be created if your exhibit space permits by setting up two folding screens, firmly anchored or propped up, to enclose a little, private place. Don't forget to include a long mirror.

Carol Sedestrom, who, along with Jo Ann Brown, owned and operated Little Jo Designs, tells a funny story about garments at a craft fair. The Little Jo line, back in 1968, consisted of a small group of loungewear, dresses and pantsuits made of fabulous Indian bedspreads. The line had been successfully selling in local stores and boutiques, and based on the good reception they decided to go into the Bennington craft fair. In preparation they re-worked their basic patterns to get the best possible fit—lowering armholes, changing the bust darts, changing the cut of the front.

At the fair they set up their display, backed up by a two-screen try-on area, and were deluged with business. Word spread through the fair, and women flocked to Little Jo. One woman in particular raved about the garments, slipped into the try-on room, and emerged happily, buying three dresses. Early the next morning, when the fair opened again the woman was back, ordering more, raving about the great fit that Carol and Jo Ann had designed.

Unfortunately the woman was wearing one of the dresses she had bought the day before. Carol and Jo Ann were horrified to see she had it on backwards, with the zipper marching down her front, the armholes skewed to the rear, and the much-worked-over bust darts gently cradling the woman's shoulder blades. After a momentary battle with honesty they thanked the woman for her compliments and sold her another outfit.

"One thing it showed us," says Carol. "No matter what you do, somebody will like it . . ."

PRICING

Pricing your item for a craft fair is different from pricing for duplicative selling to retailers. All pricing, of course, is based on totaling up your direct materials cost, your direct labor cost, your overhead expenses, and then adding an amount for profit. For craft fair selling, however, you must add in an amount that covers your own (or somebody else's) selling time, sitting behind the display table.

If you are accustomed to selling only on the wholesale level prior to the craft fair, you owe it to your retailer customers to protect them on their pricing, and maintain their price levels. Their retail mark-up includes their overhead and selling staff's salaries, so you can safely use their retail selling price as your own for the duration of the fair, remembering to add the retail sales tax, if any, onto the marked price at the time of sale.

If you have not sold much of anything before, you have to work out your own relationship between costs and profit you would like to recognize per item. Potters often have a harder time pricing than other craftspersons since the clay, glazes and kiln time are not terribly expensive, and throwing or building goes pretty fast, too. Potter Leif Wicklund offers this as his pricing formula for craft fairs—one half the selling price covers the cost of making the object, and the other half covers the cost of selling it, and includes the profit. In this way he finds he is able to get some perspective on whether or not he is making money in sufficient amounts to make it all worthwhile. Leif says he might take in a total of $100, but his pure profit would work out to be around $30. From there he can figure out how many sales he must make to be happy with the results of a craft fair.

Lest this all sound too inviting, let me point out that the competition at a craft fair is unbelievably keen, and you are elbow to elbow with your competitors. Since everybody always minds everybody else's business, a cardinal rule is to stick by your established prices whenever possible. As soon as word gets around that you are making deals you might be in for a lot of unpleasantness. Crafts are more expensive and more highly valued than mass-produced items anyway, remember?

Bob Ebendorf, metalsmith and teacher at the State University College at New Paltz, New York, cautions new participants in craft fairs to expect a relatively small volume of business for the first time in any show. Use your debut year to learn about the specific customers who come to the show, what their likes and dislikes are, the pace of the show, and what the competition is. Craft fair business is cumulative, says Bob, building up over the years as you become known as a regular, and people look forward to seeing you and your things again. Naturally, mailings to your customer list help build up your reputation.

LOCATING CRAFT FAIRS

How do you go about finding the craft fairs that are being planned for your area? The first source is the trade press for your specific field. Chances are you are already subscribing to a craft magazine such as *Hand Weaver and Craftsman, Ceramics Monthly, Shuttle, Spindle and Dyepot,* or perhaps you are receiving *Craft*

Horizons and *Outlook* along with your membership as a working craftsperson in the American Crafts Council (more about A.C.C. later).

Check your local library for the publications pertinent to your field, and re-read Chapter V of this book which contains more data on trade publications plus a partial list of the media.

Next, each state has its own State Council of the Arts, which maintains an information service about events within the state. Write to them and ask specifically that you be sent information about craft fairs scheduled for your area, and also that you be advised of any other information centers they know about that could furnish you with craft fair data.

The addresses for State Councils are listed in Appendix VII, page 219.

Other information sources not to be overlooked are the State and County Extension Service offices of the United States Department of Agriculture. These operate mainly in non-urban areas, working closely with local craftspeople in setting up marketing channels such as fairs, shows, etc. Not every local office has an active crafts program, so write to your State Extension Service office and find out where crafts programs are functioning nearest to you. Addresses are listed in Appendix VIII, page 227.

If you want further data, check your telephone book for any community arts or crafts operations in your area. Your raw materials supplier would know about these also. Check the art departments of local colleges and schools, independent craft cooperatives, the Y.M.C.A., Y.M.H.A., senior citizens centers or other studio groups, and find out if they have a folder on craft shows, or a bulletin board or newsletter that would list upcoming events. Sometimes local newspaper offices are able to furnish data on craft fairs.

REFERENCE MATERIAL

As you can gather, the craft fair/art show operation is a rather loosely organized affair, with no central information point and no national or even regional *modus operandi*. The Department of Agriculture is working to rectify this communication gap so the individual craftsperson can sometime in the near future be able to get pertinent, up-to-the-minute data on the many channels for marketing his products that are open to him.

Several excellent pieces of literature are available on crafts and craft projects from the U.S.D.A. such as:

Encouraging American Craftsmen
Co-ops—A Tool to Improve and Market Crafts
American Crafts—A Rich Heritage and
    a Rich Future
Accounting Exercise for Craft Cooperative Book-
    keepers

To get these and other pieces of literature write to: Mr. William R. Seymour, Craft Specialist, Farmer Cooperative Service, U.S. Department of Agriculture, Washington, D.C. 20250.

AMERICAN CRAFTS COUNCIL

Finally, write to the American Crafts Council and ask for information about their many programs, and for application forms that explain their different levels of membership. The Council is a unique organization —nonprofit, educational and cultural, serving a national membership from its New York headquarters since 1943. Its programs are aimed at gaining general recognition and public support of crafts, stimulating awareness of the value of the basic concept of craftsmanship and of the contribution of the individual craftsperson to an improved environment.

The Council works with State Arts Councils and government agencies along with private institutions and community groups all over the country. As a functioning organizational structure the Council has divided up the United States into six regions—Northeast, Southeast, South Central, Northwest, Southwest and North Central—each having elected assemblies and representatives. It is this structure that gives the Council a strong local base and allows it to be truly reflective of activities in all parts of the country.

The Research and Education Department of the A.C.C. is a center for information and educational services, and houses an impressive collection of pictorial and biographical information on twentieth-century American craftspeople. Slide films and movies as well as many printed publications are available either for rental or purchase. In addition, members receive a bimonthly magazine, *Craft Horizons,* and craftsmen/sustaining members receive a bimonthly newsletter, *Outlook,* full of current developments and upcoming exhibition news throughout the country.

The Museum of Contemporary Crafts is the national exhibition center of the organization, and presents a series of shows each year. Membership in the organization also includes a pass to the museum, located in New York City.

There is no parallel group to the A.C.C. in the United States today that offers as much to craftspeople who are focusing on one-of-a-kind, non-duplicative craft work. If you are not building up a volume whole-sale or retail business, you owe it to yourself to investi-gate the A.C.C. Write to: American Crafts Council, 44 West 53rd Street, New York, New York 10019.

chapter XII

Art Galleries and Mail Order

If you plan to create one-of-a-kind pieces and sell to art galleries, the whole thing is a different story. Research, licensing, production, costing, publicity—you name it, for the art world is a completely different endeavor from setting yourself up to duplicate your own original designs for retailers or for direct customers.

To begin with, it's much harder. The outlets are fewer and the competition is keen. Not to say that the wholesale/retail competition is slouchy—but crafts are the stepchildren of the gallery world and must compete not only with other crafts but also with the paintings and prints that comprise most of the galleries' exhibits.

Your chances of making money are a lot slimmer in the fine art market than in cadging small orders from store buyers and interested consumers. Also the timing is longer, and might run from a month or two up to a year or two from acceptance on consignment in a gallery to your receipt of the actual payment for the piece.

176

ART GALLERIES

If the above paragraphs haven't knocked you out of the field, let's explore how you approach gallery selling. Step one is to figure out what makes you think your craft items border on fine art rather than on fine craft. Wise men and women through the ages have attempted to define what is art and what is not art, and since no conclusion has ever been reached by the sages I don't feel compelled at all to deal with the question. Let it suffice to say that the dividing line is a fine one, and that it seems to change with the decades. A wall hanging displayed and sold in a shop may or may not be any more a work of art than a wall hanging displayed in a gallery.

The best way to get a handle on the question of art versus non-art is to spend some time studying the contents of the galleries near to you. Galleries are similar to retail stores in that each has a distinctive point of view, and merchandise selected to appeal to one certain segment of the population. You might find a local gallery that shows only the recognized leaders in the current art scene, or one that deals solely in one certain time period of art. Others will specialize in contemporary artists or certain categories of work such as litho or watercolor.

A gallery, like all other businesses, is set up to make money in some manner—either directly, as a result of successful selling, or as a tax loss write-off for citizens in the higher income brackets. This aspect alone makes a gallery a unique operation, with "angels" or backers picking up the tab for the rent and maintenance, allowing the titular head of the gallery freedom from the more mundane cares of the day. Also the timing of cash flow for a gallery can be much laxer than for a retail store where every square foot of space must earn its keep in sales dollars every week.

Most galleries are "stable" galleries, meaning that the owner/manager puts together a group of artists whose conglomerate output is attractive to the ideal customer of the gallery, and whose work is relatively complementary to each other. Gaining acceptance as part of a stable gives the artist a home base and a certain amount of stability in that his work will be regularly exhibited, a condition devoutly to be desired. Other galleries, much in the minority today in the United States, are "one-shot" exhibition places that do not seek a stable of reliable contributors, but deal in whatever seems right to them at the time. Occasionally such a gallery will have a few quasi-regular exhibitors but they are not built up or developed in any way.

The time you spend in your local galleries will give you a clearer idea of what the experts in your area consider to be an art work rather than a craft piece—a definition you need to become familiar with. Gallery owners feel that this definition is not well enough understood by craftspeople. Ms. Maggie Tripp, former co-owner of Philadelphia's Gallery 252, cautions, "Train yourself to think in terms of small quantities of exceptional work that will not be found around the corner in the Peasant Shop."

Her emphasis on the word "exceptional" is important. Just doing fine work is not enough. Fine work finds its place in boutique shops and specialty corners in larger stores. Exceptional work, a piece that makes a statement, is unique in its own way, might have a future in a gallery. The ability to judge what is and is not gallery material comes only with exposure to gallery shows and study of the field.

Publications such as *Art News, Art in America* and

Craft Horizons, to name a few, will be helpful in defining what is suitable for exhibition. All these periodicals will show you what is being hailed as pace-setting in galleries across the country.

GALLERY PIECES VERSUS RETAIL ITEMS

The difference between gallery work and retail store and boutique items cannot be stressed too much. Designers working in each of these directions approach their task differently and come out with completely opposite end results. As you have seen in the preceding chapters of this book, designing for duplicative sales is much less an art than a case of excellent skills coupled with knowledge of the market and an ability to trim down the creative urge to where it fits the supply and demand of the buyer. "If the big color is red, you make it red," and "There are just so many ways to set in a sleeve" are the obbligatos of the design-to-sell-volume theme.

Not so with the fine artist/craftsperson. Ms. Deborah Aquado, a recognized contemporary goldsmith who heads up the Crafts Department at New York's New School for Social Research, feels that the word "integrated" is the key to the artist's approach. The artist/craftsperson ideally is unencumbered by restrictions of time, money, trends and other commercial points. This sort of freedom permits complete integration between materials and the craftsperson's projection of the object. In simpler language, the craftsperson feels a rapport with his chosen material and that mostly is what influences the creation, with little or no thought to price level and/or salability. Much the same as fine artists have been doing down through the centuries.

It's all a different world. If you end up after careful

study of local galleries, publications and contemporary museum collections concluding that your things belong in a retail store environment, then go there and save the galleries for an enrichment of yourself rather than as a possible sales outlet. You might find that as time passes and your skill and point of view change, a second consideration of gallery exhibitions is in the cards for you. Per usual, honesty is the top requirement in self-evaluation.

RELATIONSHIP OF THE ARTIST TO HIS WORK

The emotional relationship between an artist/craftsperson and his work is different from that of the commercial designer. A piece of fine art is actually an extention of the artist, a representation of where and what that person is at the moment, an exposure of the private inner world of the artist. Since each object is a totally personal expression, a strong bond continues to exist even after the piece is sold. Each curve and plane of the piece is tactilely familiar to the creator as each part of a baby's tiny body is familiar to the loving parent. Protective feelings are inevitable.

A story illustrating this point is told by Debby Aguado about a ring she had made for an exhibition at the now-defunct America House gallery. Debby was working in silver at the time, and had designed a wonderful, sculptural wedding band. Shortly after the exhibit opened Debby received a call from America House saying they had a customer who wanted the ring, but in gold rather than in silver. She agreed, produced the gold ring and delivered it pronto.

Months passed, and one day Debby was in Cartier's, the New York jewelers, on business. Seated nearby was an attractive, well-dressed woman whose hands were covered with rings of all sorts. Debby cast a professional eye on the collection and was delighted to spot her sculptured gold baby on one of the woman's fingers. The ring looked really great, far outshining the rest of the jewelry, so Debby spoke up, convinced that the woman would be tickled pink to meet the creator in the flesh.

She leaned over and, to open the conversation, asked where the woman had purchased the gold ring. The woman waved her hand in front of Debby and announced loftily that she had designed it herself. Stunned, Debby hesitated a moment and then fled the store, filled with incredible rage. How dare this creature make claim to her work? She, who had fashioned it lovingly? It took her many weeks to calm down, and she now discusses it laughingly, fully aware how emotionally loaded the topic is for her and for other artists.

LOCATING A GALLERY

Shopping for which gallery would be right for your designs is a lot different from shopping around to see which retail stores you want to contact and show to. The gallery selection is limited outside of larger cities and cultural centers, and only a portion of functioning galleries are interested in crafts to begin with. Check as many galleries personally as you can.

The competition is unbelievable for the few spots within those few galleries. Everyone fresh out of art school heads for the galleries along with hobbyists, local artists and craftspeople, art teachers, print makers and related commercial art people such as graphics designers and lithographers. The chances of having items accepted for exhibition are very small, considering the hordes of talented, well-intentioned, would-be exhibitors. Artist Ed Plunkett, of the Graham Gallery, laughingly compares the gallery seekers to people dashing off to Hollywood and expecting to get into the movies! The comparison, unfortunately, is a valid one.

APPOINTMENTS

However, if you are determined to give it a try, and have worked out an understanding of the point of view of a gallery or two you feel your work would fit in to, then go to it. The initial contact is more often made in person than by phone or letter. Galleries generally open in the late morning, and the before-noon hour is a good time to put in an appearance, asking for the owner. Identify yourself and your skill area and say you would like a few minutes to show your things. Expect to be asked to come back at some later time, though, and don't take it personally. You might also be told that the gallery is filled for the next few months and be asked to come back after that time.

PRESENTING YOUR WORK

The presentation of pieces to the gallery owner, whenever it actually takes place, is much lower keyed than showing to a retail store buyer. Expect to spend some time with the owner, establishing rapport. Color slides are the accepted way of showing pieces, with several smaller sample works brought along to illustrate the manner in which the actual item is done, finished, and how it looks and feels inside, outside and upside down.

If your slides kindle interest, you might be asked to leave them at the gallery for further consideration. Accept the offer gracefully if it happens. It is perfectly safe to leave things at a reputable gallery. You will not be copied, or "knocked off" since your work is a personal extension of you and could not be duplicated by the owner's friends or relatives even if they wanted to.

Bring anywhere from six to a dozen slides with you at a time. The gallery owner will be well able to get an idea of your work and know if it is or is not his cup of tea. If you have personal credentials that are pertinent to the gallery scene it is smart to mention them, but your slides are basically what speak for you rather than the fact you teach textile design in a nearby school. Since slides are the accepted presentation form you need not carry your own viewer with you. They will have one on the premises, and chances are it will be larger and clearer than the hand types.

Sometimes the gallery contact happens easily, naturally, and once in a while, totally by mistake. Painter Bob Blust, who is co-owner of a New York advertising agency, was asked by an artist friend to come along and give him moral support on the artist's first gallery appointment. Armed with the man's slides, they went in, met the owner and proceeded to have an interesting discussion about art. The gallery owner finally turned down Bob's friend's work, feeling it wouldn't be right for his clients.

As they all walked to the door Bob mentioned that he painted a bit in his spare time. The owner invited him to come back and show a few things that he had done. The result was, of course, that Bob's canvases were accepted immediately and he's been a part of that gallery's stable ever since, turning out new works on weekends and holidays.

CONSIGNMENT

Estimates vary on the exact figure, but an educated guess would place 75 percent of all gallery items as being on consignment, and 25 percent as outright purchases. Naturally the larger or very expensive pieces will be almost totally consignment, so the outright purchases fall into lower priced work. Sometimes, too, a gallery owner will be able to get a really good buy on a small group of less expensive pieces that are a sure bet for one of his regular clients, and direct sale money will be offered. Still, better expect that consignment will be the arrangement offered to you. Be sure you get a receipt for all consignment items, with a detailed description of each one, for your own protection.

PRICING

Have a firm figure in mind for your price before you ever set foot in the gallery. Gallery mark-ups vary on category and location but the figure of 40 percent crops up regularly. The gallery mark-up is tacked onto your selling price, and is what the client pays. No discounting is involved between you and the gallery and you can expect to receive your check at the end of the month in which the piece was sold.

How do you set a price on your gallery pieces? There is no formula similar to the one for costing production items, but certain general guidelines may be helpful. You still want to keep in mind your own labor cost, your direct materials cost, and some type of profit mark-up for yourself. Did Michelangelo have an hourly rate? It's doubtful, but he certainly must have had some idea of what he thought his time and talent were worth. And of the profit he needed to realize to make it all worthwhile.

Each craftsperson must establish his own market level in response to his own needs. But the market level must also be in keeping with the rest of the local craft/art community. If one designer so underprices his work that it jeopardizes the other designers in his area he is not being a responsible creator. So, concurrent with figuring the costs of labor, material and profit percentage, shop around the area carefully and see what general price range other artists place their work in. Since you are dealing in one-of-a-kind work you will not be able to get definitive prices out of your shopping tours but you should be able to see average categorical prices for small sculpture, jewelry, leatherwork, etc.

BUSINESS ARRANGEMENTS

Before you leave the gallery be sure you understand exactly what you receive from them in dollars when your work is sold, and the amount of time it usually takes them to issue their checks to the artists. If this information is not included on your copy of the consignment receipt it is acceptable form to jot it down right there so no ugly situations can ever develop. Also it is smart to ask how many months your work will be kept by the gallery if it is not sold. On new people's work the time seems to vary between six months and two years.

EXPENSES

If a gallery accepts your work you might find you are asked to pay your share of expenses for a show or an opening. A catalog must be compiled and printed, invitations printed, addressed and mailed out, refreshments purchased, and so forth.

Whether or not you will be expected to pick up part of the tab depends to a large extent on the part of the United States you are showing in, and the type of show.

Geographically, galleries on the two coasts seem more prone to charge than galleries in the middle of the country. Since you are just starting out you will doubtless be part of a group show that includes other artists. Your share of the expenses of an opening might be figured proportionately to the number of pieces you have in the show. Or it might be figured out on any number of other formulas. If this happens, find out how the charges are figured. None of the amounts would be very large, and any activity that brings the public into the gallery adds to your chances of having a client buy one of your pieces.

In summary, it is best not to look on gallery selling as a purely money-making proposition. If it works for you, fine. If not, you can try to combine it with other ventures. Gallery audiences are a bit different from any other customers who might want to buy your things. People buy art works for many different reasons. One, highly touted in America today, is the theory that with a certain amount of taste and research a person can discover unknown artists, buy their works for a song, hold them for a decade, and have a truly valuable investment that will pay off at time of sale. How much of this actually happens is debatable.

Other people buy art work because they genuinely like the piece or because they need it. A case of need is illustrated in Maggie Tripp's story about the first customer she ever had at her Gallery 252. Maggie, a gracious, charming Philadelphia woman, opened up on Day One at about eleven in the morning, as excited as could be. At about eleven-thirty a man dressed in greasy coveralls marched in and asked, "Do you sell paintings, lady?"

Maggie admitted she did, and the man told her a lengthy tale about a "great new chick, really stacked" that he had recently become involved with.

It seems that he had wanted to impress the new lady

friend, so he had offered to wallpaper her living room. Unfortunately he had miscalculated on the amount of wallpaper needed for the job. He had completed the papering and had ended up with an unpapered rectangle about 2 feet by 3 feet in the middle of one wall. In order to pacify the New Babe he had grandly announced he would buy her a painting to cover up the hole.

Maggie sympathetically asked how much he was prepared to spend on his gift. The man turned his coverall pockets inside out and together they counted out $36.83.

"You want a print, not a painting," said Maggie, leading him to the print area. Green was his color, he declared—perhaps something with trees. At length the perfect tree print was located, large enough to cover the missing wallpaper.

As she was wrapping the print up Maggie told the man he was lucky, the print only cost $25.00. He leaned over, patted her arm and said, "You been swell, lady, you really helped me out. You mark down the twenty-five on the books, and get yourself a little something with the rest."

MAIL ORDER SELLING

The other alternate marketing area that might be of interest to you is selling by mail. It looks pretty easy, neatly bypasses the difficulties and pressures of dealing with buyers or directly with the public, and seems to offer a larger potential customer group than word-of-mouth referrals. However, it is also a complex business activity all its own, highly competitive and extremely hazardous to the newcomer.

Mail order selling requires lots of organization, hours of maintenance to be profitable, and is slow to build up into really good money levels. Extra capital is required for printing, postage, mailing lists or advertisements, above and beyond the capital you need to get your designs off the ground.

RESEARCH

Before making any move toward direct mail selling, scout the market thoroughly. Study the ads in the back of magazines and newspapers, send for the space rates and mechanical requirements for placing advertising in any publications that look as if they carry ads for products similar in feeling to yours. Check all mail order catalogs you and your friends have received to see the type and price range of items offered. Check and see what books your local library has on direct mail or mail order selling. The more information you get, the better.

SUITABILITY

Then study your line and see how your designs relate to mail order selling. Are they really very different-looking from items that can be found in most retail stores? People seldom bother to send away for things they can go out and buy locally. Is your work dependent on eye appeal, i.e., great colors or textures? Chances are it is not slated for success in direct mail since neither color nor texture reproduces well in small ads or mailing pieces.

Determine how easy it would be to mail your items, and check the costs of mailing-boxes, paper, etc. Look into the special needs of shipping breakables.

COSTING

Costing for direct mail is figured differently from costing for straight wholesaling or retailing since additional expenses are involved in the mail order process.

The U.S. Small Business Administration offers a costing formula in its excellent bulletin titled "Selling By Mail Order."

Merchandise must be offered at an attractive price; yet that price should be set at a level which will provide an adequate profit. A good formula is to divide each dollar of expected sales into three parts: one-third for cost of merchandise, one-third for operating costs including selling expense, and one-third for wages and profit for the owner. For example, if an item costs 50 cents from the supplier, the sales price should be $1.50. If the mark-up, and resulting sales price, appear higher than for a retail store, it must be remembered that finding prospects is an expense that must be included as part of the selling price.

TAXES

Achieving legitimacy is relatively easy. To date, no permits or licenses are required to operate a mail order business, but the tax structures are different from retailing or wholesaling. For example, federal excise taxes are imposed on certain items, etc. Write and get the regulations for mail order from: U.S. Department of the Treasury, 15th Street and Pennsylvania Avenue N.W., Washington, D.C. 20220.

And, since you are selling direct to the customer be sure to get copies of your state and local tax regulations. See the list of state tax commission names and addresses in Appendix I, page 199. Understand what is expected of you before you make a sale via the mails.

MAILING LISTS

Mailing lists may be rented or purchased from mailing list companies in major cities all over the United

States. Check the yellow pages of the largest city near you to see what an amazing variety of consumer categories are available to you. They are bought or rented at so much per name or per thousand names, and are categorized as to mail order use. The more selective the list is, the higher the cost. For example, a list of licensed dog owners per state would have a different price from a list of high school seniors.

A good return from the general mailing list, i.e., not very specific as to category, is about 2 percent response out of the total number mailed out. The more selective the list, the higher the expected response, up to between 5 and 10 percent.

Lists rented for limited use generally have a number of phony names included that help the list owners keep track of whether or not you have copied their list and are using it without paying them a second time. Other mailing list houses insist you furnish them with your mailing material and they do the actual addressing and sending out, without your ever coming in contact with their lists. Some organizations offer the use of their own lists as a courtesy to their members. Shop around and see what you have to choose from.

The maintenance of a mailing list must be an on-going effort to make it really pay off. If you purchase a list outright you must constantly weed out non-responders, and introduce new names from additional lists.

POSTAL REGULATIONS

Check with your Post Office for local regulations on direct mail. There are a few facts you might not know about the regular mail service which suddenly become important when dealing in quantity:

First Class Mail: May be sealed; will be forwarded to a new address or returned to the sender if unclaimed. Most expensive way of mailing anything.

Third or Fourth Class Mail: Will not be forwarded or returned unless the sender indicates he will cover the additional postal charges by writing on the mailer "Return Postage Guaranteed" or "Forwarding and Return Postage Guaranteed." Costs less than first class mail.

Address Correction: The sender can write "Address Correction Requested" on the letter and he will receive the address to which the mail was forwarded or will be told the reason why his letter could not be delivered. Since this is pretty involved there is a charge of ten cents per correction request. This service is available on first, third and fourth class mail.

While you are at your Post Office be sure to register your own business name with them if it is different from your own name so any mail that comes in will definitely get delivered to you.

FRAUDULENT USE OF THE MAILS

Other bits of information to be aware of when dealing in mail order are the regulations defining the fraudulent use of the U.S. mails. This sometimes happens quite innocently. The most common cause of fraud charges in mail order selling is lack of delivery. For example, say you receive an order with payment enclosed. If there is any delay in your mailing back the merchandise, the customer might get impatient and report you to the postal authorities, charging fraudulent use of the mails. This can cause no end of trouble and can result in your being investigated.

Be extremely careful, too, about any claims you make about your products. When fraudulent, excessive advertising is done through the mails you must answer to the postal authorities. When done in newspaper and magazine advertising you must answer to the Federal Trade Commission, who have very strong rulings about truth in advertising. State only the honest facts and take care not to omit pertinent information that might affect the sale. The sin of omission is as great as the sin of commission, according to the F.T.C.

SPACE ADVERTISING

If you decide to run a series of ads in magazines or newspapers rather than buying or renting mailing lists, shop around for the less expensive publications for your initial attempts. The library will have lists of all the smaller publications issued in the United States. Check these lists for what might be good media in which to test the field and gain experience, rather than aiming right away at the big money books. Many company magazines and trade publications have excellent direct mail records.

After you have assembled several likely publications, make up one advertisement that can be placed in all of them. Code each ad by placing a key number or letter someplace in the return coupon so you will be able to judge which magazine or paper brought you which responses. In this way you can judge which of the publications is doing the best selling job for your products, and at what cost per item. Smart direct mail people are constantly revising their media schedules to find the ultimate combinations of magazines and newspapers.

REFERENCE

As you can see, mail order selling is a whole separate field, with very definite rules that govern success or failure. You might want to write to some of the direct mail trade associations and request information about the field and about their organization. Several of the trade associations are:

Associated Third Class Mail Users
1725 K Street N.W.
Washington, D.C. 20006

Direct Mail Advertisers Association
230 Park Avenue
New York, New York 10017

Mail Order Association of America
612 N. Michigan Street
Chicago, Illinois 60611

MAILINGS AS A SELLING AID

Lest all this discourage you, I firmly believe that direct mail can be used very effectively as an adjunct to other types of selling. If, for example, you have built up a small personal mailing list from your participation in craft fairs and art shows, you would be very right in making up a one-page mailing piece with photos or sketches, descriptions and prices, plus a "tear off and return" coupon. Keep it simple and to the point—remember, these are people who have already purchased and enjoyed your things. Just give the facts, in an attractive manner. Photo-offset is an ideal printing process for mailers, so check your phone book for offset printing houses in your area. If you can do clear, pleasant sketches, however, even a mimeographed sheet might suffice.

Unless the postage is prohibitive, enclose copies of any publicity write-ups you've been able to get. Past customers usually are delighted to get this kind of information, and feel like one of the family.

Send the mailers out, and enjoy extra sales without getting involved with other people's mailing lists, extra money and extra labor.

This type of mailing can be used to good effect on the wholesale level as well. Lists of stores and galleries are available, such as the fine booklet published by the American Crafts Council, "Craft Shops/Galleries U.S.A." This publication is available by mail at nominal cost, and describes the craft categories and purchasing policies of over one thousand businesses that market American crafts.

And for women craftspeople ONLY—Know, Inc., a women's publishing collective whose delightful slogan proclaims "Freedom of the Press Belongs to Those Who Own the Press," publishes a list of craft shops, galleries and other retail outlets either run by women or interested in promoting items made by women. Copies are available by mail at modest cost.

Know, Inc., also publishes a Christmas gift catalog of women's products. As their Christmas gift to all women, the catalog ads are free, and just require camera-ready copy to be sent in to them four months before the holidays. Copy size must be $3\frac{3}{4}''$ x $4\frac{1}{4}''$.

A painless way to produce camera-ready copy is to draw out the dimensions of the ad on plain paper, and then type, letter, and sketch the ad exactly as you want it to run. If you want to include a photo, paste it in, but be sure it is quite light because photos reproduce darker than the original. Be sure to include clear directions for ordering your items!

The Christmas Catalog is sent out to over two thousand readers, and circulation is growing. If you would like to include a small donation to Know, Inc., as your Christmas gift to activist women you can write it off on your income tax since the organization has a tax-exempt status. But donation or no, send your copy in early to: Know, Inc., P.O. Box 86031, Pittsburgh, Pennsylvania 15221.

Things to Keep in Mind: A Summary

It's hard to summarize a factual how-to-do-it book since facts can't really be summarized, except as formulas to write on cuffs before taking an exam. I can, though, reiterate some of the concepts which this book is based upon with the hope that you will find them helpful:

Be honest with yourself in evaluating designs, estimating progress or planning future moves.

If you don't understand something, keep asking until it's clear enough *to explain to somebody else.*

Send for copies of all the rules and regulations so you can read, understand and follow them, or at least know which laws you are bending and straining.

Do your costing even though it's hateful.

196

Do some publicity even though it's embarrassing.

Be gentle with yourself. What you are doing is very difficult and nobody will know it but you.

.

Appendices

Appendix I:

STATE DEPARTMENTS OF TAXATION AND REVENUE

ALABAMA:

State of Alabama
Department of Revenue
Use Tax Division
Montgomery, Alabama 36102

ALASKA:

State of Alaska
Department of Revenue
P.O. Box 3-3000
Pouch S A, Juneau, Alaska 99801

ARIZONA:

State Tax Commission of Arizona
Sales Tax Division
1700 West Washington, House
  Wing
Phoenix, Arizona 85007

ARKANSAS:

Arkansas State Tax Bureau
Little Rock, Arkansas 72201

CALIFORNIA:

State of California
State Board of Equalization
1020 N Street, P.O. Box 1799
Sacramento, California 95808

COLORADO:

Colorado State Department of
  Revenue
Sales Tax Section
State Capitol Annex
1375 Sherman Street
Denver, Colorado 80203

CONNECTICUT:

State of Connecticut
Tax Department
92 Farmington Avenue
Hartford, Connecticut 06115

DELAWARE:

State of Delaware
Department of Finance
Division of Revenue
601 Delaware Avenue
Wilmington, Delaware 19899

FLORIDA:

State of Florida
Department of Revenue
Tallahassee, Florida 32304

199

GEORGIA:

As long as a person works out of his home he is considered to be a consumer, and thus required to pay all taxes on goods purchased. When he establishes a separate place of business he must apply for a license. Write to:

State of Georgia

Department of Revenue
Sales and Use Tax Unit
Trinity Washington Building
Atlanta, Georgia 30334

HAWAII:

State of Hawaii
Department of Taxation
P.O. Box 259
Honolulu, Hawaii 96809

IDAHO:

Idaho State Tax Commission
Box 36
371 Main Street
Boise, Idaho 83707

ILLINOIS:

State of Illinois
Department of Revenue
Springfield, Illinois 62708

INDIANA:

State of Indiana
Department of Revenue
State Office Building
Indianapolis, Indiana 46204

IOWA:

State of Iowa
Department of Revenue
Lucas State Office Building
Des Moines, Iowa 50319

KANSAS:

Kansas State Department of
    Revenue
Division of Taxation
Topeka, Kansas 66625

KENTUCKY:

Commonwealth of Kentucky
Department of Revenue
Frankfort, Kentucky 40601

LOUISIANA:

State of Louisiana
Department of Revenue
Baton Rouge, Louisiana 70821

MAINE:

State of Maine
Bureau of Taxation
Augusta, Maine 04330

MARYLAND:

State of Maryland
Comptroller of the Treasury
Retail Sales Tax Division
301 West Preston Street
Baltimore, Maryland 21201

MASSACHUSETTS:

Commonwealth of Massachusetts
Department of Corporations and
    Taxation
Sales and Use Tax Division
P.O. Box 7010
Boston, Massachusetts 02204

MICHIGAN:

State of Michigan
Department of Treasury
Treasury Building
Lansing, Michigan 48922

MINNESOTA:

Minnesota Department of
Taxation
Sales and Use Tax Division
Centennial Office Building
St. Paul, Minnesota 55145

MISSISSIPPI:

Mississippi State Tax Commission
Sales and Use Tax Division
Jackson, Mississippi 39205

MISSOURI:

State of Missouri
Department of Revenue
Jefferson City, Missouri 65101

MONTANA:

Montana State Tax Bureau
Helena, Montana 59601

NEBRASKA:

State of Nebraska
Department of Revenue
Lincoln, Nebraska 68509

NEVADA:

Nevada State Tax Commission
Carson City, Nevada 89701

NEW HAMPSHIRE:

This state has no sales tax, no
required state permits or licenses,
and no exemption certificates are
needed. However, New Hampshire does have a Business Profits
Tax which you should inquire
about when and if your business
gets sizable. Write to:

State of New Hampshire
Tax Commission
Concord, New Hampshire 03301

NEW JERSEY:

New Jersey Department of the
Treasury
Division of Taxation
West State and Willow Streets
Trenton, New Jersey 08625

NEW MEXICO:

State of New Mexico
Bureau of Revenue
P.O. Box 630
Santa Fe, New Mexico 87501

NEW YORK:

New York State Department of
Taxation and Finance
State Campus
Albany, New York 12227

NORTH CAROLINA:

State of North Carolina
Department of Revenue
Raleigh, North Carolina 27622

NORTH DAKOTA:

North Dakota Tax Department
State Capitol
Bismarck, North Dakota 58501

OHIO:

State of Ohio
Department of Taxation
68 East Gay Street
Columbus, Ohio 43215

OKLAHOMA:

Oklahoma State Tax Commission
2101 Lincoln Boulevard
Oklahoma City, Oklahoma 73194

OREGON:

Oregon has no sales or use taxes
so no permits, licenses or exemption certificates are required on
the state level. However, there is
a corporation income and excise
tax, so if you are headed toward
incorporating write to:

State of Oregon
Department of Revenue
State Office Building
Salem, Oregon 97310

PENNSYLVANIA:

Commonwealth of Pennsylvania
Department of Revenue
Bureau of Taxes for Education
1846 Brookwood Street
Harrisburg, Pennsylvania 17128

RHODE ISLAND:

State of Rhode Island
Department of Administration
Division of Taxation, Sales Tax
  Section
289 Promenade Street
Providence, Rhode Island 02901

SOUTH CAROLINA:

South Carolina State Tax
  Commission
P.O. Box 125
Columbia, South Carolina 29214

SOUTH DAKOTA:

South Dakota State Department
  of Revenue
State Capitol Building
Pierre, South Dakota 57501

TENNESSEE:

State of Tennessee
Department of Revenue
Andrew Jackson State Office
  Building
Nashville, Tennessee 37242

TEXAS:

State of Texas
Comptroller of Public Accounts
Drawer S S, Capitol Station
Austin, Texas 78711

UTAH:

Utah State Tax Commission
Salt Lake City, Utah 84114

VERMONT:

State of Vermont
Department of Taxes, Sales and
  Use Tax Division
P.O. Box 547
Montpelier, Vermont 05602

VIRGINIA:

Commonwealth of Virginia
Department of Taxation, Sales
  and Use Tax Division
P.O. Box 6-L
Richmond, Virginia 23215

WASHINGTON:

Washington State Department of
  Revenue
Olympia, Washington 98504

WEST VIRGINIA:

State of West Virginia
State Tax Commission
Charleston, West Virginia 25330

WISCONSIN:

State of Wisconsin
Department of Revenue
Income, Sales, Inheritance and
  Excise Tax Division
Compliance Section
P.O. Box 39
Madison, Wisconsin 53701

WYOMING:

State of Wyoming
Tax Commission
Department of Revenue
2200 Carey Avenue
Cheyenne, Wyoming 82001

Appendix II:

SMALL BUSINESS ADMINISTRATION FIELD OFFICES

ALABAMA

908 South 20th Street
Birmingham, Alabama 35205

ALASKA

1016 West Sixth Avenue
Anchorage, Alaska 99501

503 Third Avenue
Fairbanks, Alaska 99701

Federal Building
Juneau, Alaska 99801

ARIZONA

122 North Central Avenue
Phoenix, Arizona 85004

Federal Building
155 East Alameda Street
Tucson, Arizona 85701

ARKANSAS

377 P.O. & Courthouse Building
600 West Capitol Avenue
Little Rock, Arkansas 72201

CALIFORNIA

Federal Building
1130 "O" Street
Fresno, California 93721

849 South Broadway
Los Angeles, California 90014

532 North Mountain Avenue
San Bernardino, California 92401

110 West "C" Street
San Diego, California 92101

Federal Building
450 Golden Gate Avenue
San Francisco, California 94102

COLORADO

721 19th Street
Denver, Colorado 80202

CONNECTICUT

Federal Office Building
450 Maine Street
Hartford, Connecticut 06103

DELAWARE

901 Market Street
Wilmington, Delaware 19801

FLORIDA

Federal Office Building
400 West Bay Street
Jacksonville, Florida 32202

Federal Building
51 S.W. 1st Avenue
Miami, Florida 33130

Federal Building
500 Zack Street
Tampa, Florida 33602

GEORGIA

1401 Peachtree Street N.E.
Atlanta, Georgia 30309

GUAM

Ada Plaza Center Building
Agana, Guam 96910

HAWAII

1149 Bethel Street
Honolulu, Hawaii 96813

IDAHO

216 North Eighth Street
Boise, Idaho 83701

ILLINOIS

Federal Office Building
219 South Dearborn Street
Chicago, Illinois 60604

502 Monroe Street
Springfield, Illinois 62701

INDIANA

36 South Pennsylvania Street
Indianapolis, Indiana 46204

IOWA

New Federal Building
210 Walnut Street
Des Moines, Iowa 50309

KANSAS

120 South Market Street
Wichita, Kansas 67202

KENTUCKY

Federal Office Building
600 Federal Place
Louisville, Kentucky 40202

LOUISIANA

124 Camp Street
New Orleans, Louisiana 70130

MAINE

Federal Building
U.S. Post Office
40 Western Avenue
Augusta, Maine 04330

MARYLAND

1113 Federal Building
Hopkins Plaza
Baltimore, Maryland 21201

MASSACHUSETTS
John Fitzgerald Kennedy Federal
   Building
Boston, Massachusetts 02203

326 Appleton Street
Holyoke, Massachusetts 01040

MICHIGAN

1249 Washington Boulevard
Detroit, Michigan 48226

201 McClellan Street
Marquette, Michigan 49855

MINNESOTA

12 South Sixth Street
Minneapolis, Minnesota 55402

MISSISSIPPI

2500 14th Street
Gulfport, Mississippi 39501

245 East Capitol Street
Jackson, Mississippi 39205

MISSOURI

911 Walnut Street
Kansas City, Missouri 64106

Federal Building
210 North 12th Street
St. Louis, Missouri 63101

MONTANA

Power Block Building
Main & Sixth Avenue
Helena, Montana 59601

NEBRASKA

Federal Building
215 North 17th Street
Omaha, Nebraska 68102

NEVADA

300 Las Vegas Boulevard South
Las Vegas, Nevada 89101

NEW HAMPSHIRE

55 Pleasant Street
Concord, New Hampshire 03301

NEW JERSEY

970 Broad Street
Room 1636
Newark, New Jersey 07102

NEW MEXICO

Federal Building
500 Gold Avenue, S.W.
Albuquerque, New Mexico 87101

1015 El Paso Road
Las Cruces, New Mexico 88001

NEW YORK

91 State Street
Albany, New York 11297

Federal Building
Room 9, 121 Ellicott Street
Buffalo, New York 14203

26 Federal Plaza
Room 3930
New York, New York 10007

55 St. Paul Street
Rochester, New York 14604

Hunter Plaza
Fayette & Salina Streets
Syracuse, New York 13202

NORTH CAROLINA

Addison Building
222 South Church Street
Charlotte, North Carolina 28202

NORTH DAKOTA

653 Second Avenue North
Fargo, North Dakota 58102

OKLAHOMA

30 North Hudson Street
Oklahoma City, Oklahoma 73102

OHIO

5026 Federal Building
550 Main Street
Cincinnati, Ohio 45202

1240 East 9th Street
Cleveland, Ohio 44199

50 West Gay Street
Columbus, Ohio 43215

OREGON

921 Southwest Washington Street
Portland, Oregon 97205

PENNSYLVANIA

1 Decker Square
Bala Cynwyd, Pennsylvania 19004

Federal Building
1000 Liberty Avenue
Pittsburgh, Pennsylvania 15222

PUERTO RICO

255 Ponce De Leon Avenue
Hato Rey, Puerto Rico 00919

RHODE ISLAND

702 Smith Building
57 Eddy Street
Providence, Rhode Island 02903

SOUTH CAROLINA

1801 Assembly Street
Columbia, South Carolina 29201

SOUTH DAKOTA

National Bank Building
Eighth and Main Avenue
Sioux Falls, South Dakota 57102

TENNESSEE

502 South Gay Street
Knoxville, Tennessee 37902

Federal Building
167 North Main Street
Memphis, Tennessee 38103

500 Union Street
Nashville, Tennessee 37219

TEXAS

701 North Upper Broadway
Corpus Christi, Texas 78401

1100 Commerce Street
Dallas, Texas 75202

109 North Oregon Street
El Paso, Texas 79901

219 East Jackson Street
Harlingen, Texas 78550

808 Travis Street
Houston, Texas 77002

1205 Texas Avenue
Lubbock, Texas 79408

505 East Travis Street
Marshall, Texas 75670

301 Broadway
San Antonio, Texas 78205

UTAH

2237 Federal Building
125 South State Street
Salt Lake City, Utah 84111

VERMONT

Federal Building
2nd Floor
87 State Street
Montpelier, Vermont 05601

VIRGINIA

Federal Building
400 North Eighth Street
Richmond, Virginia 23240

WASHINGTON

710 Second Avenue
Seattle, Washington 98104

Courthouse Building
Room 651
Spokane, Washington 99210

WASHINGTON, D.C.

1310 L Street, N.W.
Washington, D.C. 20417

WEST VIRGINIA

3410 Courthouse & Federal
   Building
500 Quarrier Street
Charleston, West Virginia 25301

Lowndes Bank Building
109 North Third Street
Clarksburg, West Virginia 26301

WISCONSIN

510 South Barstow Street
Eau Claire, Wisconsin 54701

25 West Main Street
Madison, Wisconsin 53703

735 West Wisconsin Avenue
Milwaukee, Wisconsin 53203

WYOMING

300 North Center Street
Casper, Wyoming 82601

Appendix III:

COMPANIES AND COUNCILS PROVIDING
FORECAST AND FABRIC INFORMATION

AMERICAN WOOL COUNCIL
1460 Broadway
New York, New York 10018

CELANESE FIBERS
  MARKETING COMPANY
522 Fifth Avenue
New York, New York 10036

COTTON, INCORPORATED
1370 Avenue of the Americas
New York, New York 10019

MONSANTO TEXTILES
  DIVISION
1114 Avenue of the Americas
New York, New York 10036

WOOL BUREAU
360 Lexington Avenue
New York, New York 10017

Appendix IV:

TRADE JOURNAL AND DIRECTORY ADDRESSES

Trade Newspapers

**BOOKS & VISUAL
DEPARTMENT CM**
Fairchild Publications, Inc.
7 East 12th Street
New York, New York 10003

CALIFORNIA APPAREL NEWS
California Fashion Publications
1011 South Los Angeles Street
Los Angeles, California 90015

CALIFORNIA STYLIST
California Fashion Publications
1011 South Los Angeles Street
Los Angeles, California 90015

DAILY NEWS RECORD
7 East 12th Street
New York, New York 10003

FASHION WEEK
Fashion Week, Inc.
1016 South Broadway Place
Los Angeles, California 90015

HOME FURNISHINGS DAILY
7 East 12th Street
New York, New York 10003

MEN'S WEEK
Fashion Week, Inc.
1016 South Broadway Place
Los Angeles, California 90015

WOMEN'S WEAR DAILY
7 East 12th Street
New York, New York 10003

Trade Directories

WORKMAN PUBLISHING
COMPANY
231 East 51st Street
New York, New York 10017

Other Better Trade Publications

(A Partial Listing)

CRAFT HORIZONS
(general crafts gallery/museum
approach—comes with mem-
bership to American Crafts
Council)
44 West 53rd Street
New York, New York 10019

NATIONAL SCULPTURE
REVIEW
250 East 51st Street
New York, New York 10022

THE CRAFTSMAN
(leathercraft)
P.O. Box 1386
Fort Worth, Texas 76101

CREATIVE CRAFTS
MAGAZINE
(general crafts hobbyists)
P.O. Drawer C
31 Arch Street
Ramsey, New Jersey 07446

CUT & SEW
(needlecrafts)
c/o Write On Publications Inc.
210 Abbot Road
East Lansing, Michigan 48823

DECORATION & CRAFT IDEAS
MADE EASY
(home furnishings)
P.O. Box 9737
Fort Worth, Texas 76107

EMBROIDERER'S JOURNAL
(embroidering and sewing)
220 5th Avenue
New York, New York 10001

GEMS & MINERALS
(jewelry and minerals)
P.O. Box 687
Mentone, California 92359

HANDWEAVER & CRAFTS-
MANS MAGAZINE
(weavers)
220 5th Avenue
New York, New York 10001

HOBBIES
(general)
1006 South Michigan Avenue
Chicago, Illinois 60605

HOME WORKSHOP
(home furnishings/furniture)
229 Park Avenue South
New York, New York 10003

LAPIDARY JOURNAL
(hobbyist, jewelry maker, gem
worker)
P.O. Box 2369
San Diego, California 92112

McCALLS NEEDLEWORK &
CRAFTS MAGAZINE
(mainly needlecrafts, hobbyists
level)
230 Park Avenue
New York, New York 10017

1001 FASHION & NEEDLE-
CRAFT IDEAS
149 5th Avenue
New York, New York 10003

POPULAR CERAMICS
(hobby ceramics)
6011 Santa Monica Boulevard
Los Angeles, California 90038

POPULAR CRAFTS
(general)
7950 Deering Avenue
Canoga Park, California 91304

POPULAR HANDCRAFTS &
HOBBIES
(general)
P.O. Box 428
Seabrook, New Hampshire 03874

POPULAR NEEDLEWORK
P.O. Box 428
Seabrook, New Hampshire 03874

QUILTERS' NEWSLETTER
Box 394
Wheatridge, Connecticut 80033

THE WORKBASKET
(needlecraft)
4251 Pennsylvania
Kansas City, Missouri 64111

ART NEWS
750 3rd Avenue
New York, New York 10017

THE AMERICAN ARTIST
165 West 46th Street
New York, New York 10036

ARTS MAGAZINE
23 East 26th Street
New York, New York 10010

DESIGN MAGAZINE
(general crafts, museum and
gallery/slant)
1100 Waterway Boulevard
Indianapolis, Indiana 46202

TODAYS ART
25 West 45th Street
New York, New York 10036

WEST ART
(West Coast art news, events and
competition non-hobbyist)
P.O. Box 1396
Auburn, California 95603

EXHIBIT
(fine and commercial art)
P.O. Box 23505
Fort Lauderdale, Florida 33307

CERAMIC SCOPE
6363 Wilshire Boulevard
Los Angeles, California 90048

CERAMICS MONTHLY
P.O. Box 4548
Columbus, Ohio 43212

THE DESIGNER
(home furnishing)
1082 Park Avenue
New York, New York 10028

ART MATERIAL TRADE
NEWS
(art and craft supplies)
119 West 57th Street
New York, New York 10028

FUSION (U.S.)
(glass blowing)
American Scientific Glassblowers
  Society
309 Georgetown Avenue
Gwinhurst, Wilmington, Delaware
19809

STAINED GLASS
Stained Glass Association of
  America
3600 University Drive
Fairfax, Virginia 22030

MODERN NEEDLECRAFT
475 5th Avenue
New York, New York 10017

ARCHITECTURAL DIGEST
(home furnishing)
680 Wilshire Place
Los Angeles, California 90005

CONTRACT MAGAZINE
(home furnishing)
Gralla Publication
7 East 43rd Street
New York, New York 10017

DESIGNER & DECORATOR
  NEWS
(home furnishing)
11 West 42nd Street
New York, New York 10022

INTERIOR DESIGN
78 East 56th Street
New York, New York 10022

INTERIORS
18 East 50th Street
New York, New York 10022

JEWELERS CIRCULAR
  KEYSTONE
600 3rd Avenue
New York, New York 10016

SHUTTLE, SPINDLE &
  DYEPOT
(weavers)
2 Northfield Road
Glen Cove, New York 11542

THE INSTRUCTOR
7 Bank Street
Danville, New York 14437

TEXTILE CRAFTS
Box 3216
Los Angeles, California 90005

NORTHWEST ART NEWS &
  VIEWS
17171 Bothwall Way, North East
Seattle, Washington 98155

NEEDLE ARTS
The Embroiderers Guild
30 East 60th Street
New York, New York 10022

Appendix V:

REGIONAL AND FIELD OFFICES OF THE UNITED STATES FEDERAL TRADE COMMISSION

FEDERAL TRADE
COMMISSION
Washington, D.C. 20580

ATLANTA REGIONAL
OFFICE
730 Peachtree Street N.E.
Room 720
Atlanta, Georgia 30308

Charlotte Field Station
623 East Trade Street
Charlotte, North Carolina 28202

Miami Field Station
995 N.W. 119th Street
Miami, Florida 33168

Oak Ridge Field Office
Federal Office Building
Oak Ridge, Tennessee 37830

BOSTON REGIONAL OFFICE
John F. Kennedy Federal Building
Government Center
Boston, Massachusetts 02203

CHICAGO REGIONAL OFFICE
Suite 1437
55 East Monroe Street
Chicago, Illinois 60603

CLEVELAND REGIONAL
OFFICE
Federal Office Building
1240 East 9th Street
Cleveland, Ohio 44199

DETROIT FIELD STATION
333 Mt. Elliott Avenue
Detroit, Michigan 48207

DALLAS REGIONAL OFFICE
500 South Ervay Street
Dallas, Texas 75201

NEW ORLEANS OFFICE
333 St. Charles Street
New Orleans, Louisiana 70130

SAN ANTONIO FIELD
*   STATION*
630 Main Street
San Antonio, Texas 78212

KANSAS CITY REGIONAL
   OFFICE
Federal Office Building
911 Walnut Street
Kansas City, Missouri 64106

DENVER FIELD STATION
Federal Office Building
1961 Stout Street
Denver, Colorado 80202

LOS ANGELES REGIONAL
   OFFICE
Federal Building
11000 Wilshire Boulevard
Los Angeles, California 90024

SAN DIEGO FIELD STATION
625 Broadway
San Diego, California

NEW YORK REGIONAL
   OFFICE
26 Federal Plaza
New York, New York 10007

BUFFALO STATION
Federal Building
111 W. Huron Street
Buffalo, New York

SAN FRANCISCO REGIONAL
   OFFICE
450 Golden Gate Avenue
San Francisco, California 94102

HONOLULU FIELD STATION
333 Queen Street
Honolulu, Hawaii 98613

SEATTLE REGIONAL OFFICE
1511 Third Avenue
Seattle, Washington 98101

WASHINGTON, D.C.
   REGIONAL OFFICE
2120 L Street N.W.
Washington, D.C. 20037

PHILADELPHIA FIELD
*   STATION*
1315 Walnut Street
Philadelphia, Pennsylvania
*   19107*

Appendix VI:

CONTRACT GUIDELINES AND MANUFACTURER'S RESUME
(For reference when using a Manufacturer's Representative)

Guidelines and Resume compliments of:

NEW YORK ASSOCIATION OF MANUFACTURERS REPRESENTATIVES
1407 Broadway
New York, New York 10018

CONTRACT GUIDELINES

Agreement between Manufacturer and Representative consists of the following terms:
1. Time period:
   a. Length of contract
   b. Renewal period
   c. Cancellation clause (60 days prior to the end of the season)
2. Territory:
   a. State specific area or territory under salesmen's jurisdiction with exclusive territorial rights.
   b. State or be advised of areas now covered by other salesmen representing the manufacturer.

216

3. Commission:
   a. Overall commission
   b. Override or bonus arrangement
   c. Arrangement where area is being covered by roadmen—split or a form of compensation.
4. Delivery:
   a. Guaranteed 85% delivery on accepted orders.
   Manufacturer must notify representative of all rejected orders within two weeks.
5. Payment:
   Commissions are to be received on or about the 10th of the month for shipments made on the 1st to 31st inclusive, of the previous month.
6. Operating expense (also may be called office, rent, or overhead expense) an estimated figure to be paid on the first of each month toward the operation of the showroom. Not to be deducted or charged against commissions due or received.
7. Draw or Advance:
   a. Draw—a set designated figure to be received each week which will be charged against commissions due.
   b. Advance—an amount to be received each week predicated on a pre-agreed percentage against accepted orders. To be charged against commissions due.
8. Samples—vary according to the company policy. Most common arrangement is to charge salesman 50% off, to be charged or deducted at the end of the season. Arrangements can be made for periodic deductions to defray the large expense at the end of the time period. Some companies may allow full deductions for samples no longer needed for display.
9. Advertising—suggest arrangements be made in advance on responsibility toward expenses incurred through the use of Buying Office sketches, magazine ads, newspaper ads and other types of advertising. This can vary with company policy.
10. Invoices—should be received at least once a week and should also be marked and noted as to full or split commissions. This will vary according to prior arrangements.

NEW YORK ASSOCIATION OF MANUFACTURERS REPRESENTATIVES
MANUFACTURER'S APPLICATION AND RESUME

NAME _____

ADDRESS _____

TELEPHONE _____ PRINCIPAL _____

CATEGORY OF LINE: (Example—Jr., Sportswear, Misses, Dresses, Etc.)

_____

_____

_____

PRICE RANGE _____

VOLUME _____

LENGTH OF TIME IN BUSINESS _____

COMMISSION RATE _____

DRAW OR ADVANCE _____ RENT _____

CONTRACT _____

SALESMEN ON ROAD (Territories Covered) _____

_____

_____

PREVIOUS NEW YORK REPRESENTATIVE _____

KEY ACCOUNTS SOLD IN NEW YORK & METROPOLITAN CITIES _____

_____

D & B RATING _____

FEATURES OF LINE & ADDITIONAL COMMENTS _____

_____

_____

NATIONALLY ADVERTISED (If Yes—Please Comment) _____

_____

Appendix VII:

STATE ARTS COUNCIL DIRECTORY

All State Arts Councils are affiliates of:

Associated Councils of the Arts
1564 Broadway
New York, New York 10036

Alabama State Council on the
Arts and Humanities

M. J. Zakrzewski
Executive Director
Suite 224, 513 Madison Avenue
Montgomery, Alabama 36104
205 269-7804

Alaska State Council on the Arts

A. James Bravar
Executive Director
Fifth Floor MacKay Building
338 Denali
Anchorage, Alaska 99501
907 279-3824

Arizona Commission on the Arts
and Humanities

Mrs. Floyd J. Tester
Executive Director
6330 North 7th Street
Phoenix, Arizona 85014
602 271-5884

Arkansas State Council on the
Arts and Humanities

Dr. Sandra Perry
Coordinator, Arts and Humanities Program
Arkansas Planning Commission
Game and Fish Commission Bldg.
Capitol Mall
Little Rock, Arkansas 72201
501 371-1211

California Arts Commission

Alberto Gallo
Executive Director
808 "O" Street
Sacramento, California 95814
916 445-1530

The Colorado Council on the Arts
and Humanities

Robert N. Sheets
Executive Director
Room 205, 1550 Lincoln Street
Denver, Colorado 80203
303 892-2617/8

Connecticut Commission on the
Arts

Anthony S. Keller
Executive Director
340 Capitol Avenue
Hartford, Connecticut 06106
203 566-4770

Delaware State Arts Council

Sophie Consagra
Executive Director
601 Delaware Avenue
Wilmington, Delaware 19801
302 654-3159

District of Columbia Commission
on the Arts

Leroy Washington, III
Executive Director
Room 543, Munsey Building
1329 "E" Street, N.W.
Washington, D.C. 20004
202 629-5123/4

Fine Arts Council of Florida

Beverly Dozier
Director, Division of Cultural Affairs
Department of State
The Capitol Building
Tallahassee, Florida 32304
904 488-2416/17/18/19

Georgia Council for the Arts

George Beattie, Jr.
Executive Director
706 Peachtree Center South
225 Peachtree Street, N.E.
Atlanta, Georgia 30303
404 656-3990 - Office
404 355-3506 - Home

Hawaii—The State Foundation on
Culture and the Arts

Alfred Preis
Executive Director
Room 310, 250 South King Street
Honolulu, Hawaii 96813
808 536-7081

Idaho State Commission on the
Arts and Humanities

Suzanne D. Taylor
Executive Director
P. O. Box 577
Boise, Idaho 83701
208 384-2119

Illinois Arts Council

S. Leonard Pas, Jr.
Executive Director
Room 1610, 111 North Wabash
Ave.
Chicago, Illinois 60602
312 793-3520

Indiana Arts Commission

John M. Bitterman
Executive Director
Room 815, Thomas Building
15 East Washington Street
Indianapolis, Indiana 46204
317 633-5649

Iowa State Arts Council

Jack E. Olds
Executive Director
State Capitol Building
Des Moines, Iowa 50319
515 281-5297

Kansas Cultural Arts Commission

Robert A. Moon
Executive Director
120 North Oliver
Wichita, Kansas 67208
316 686-7411

Kentucky Arts Commission

James Edgy
Executive Director
400 Wapping Street
Frankfort, Kentucky 40601
502 564-3757

Louisiana Council for Music and
   Performing Arts

Mrs. Edwin H. Blum, President
Suite 912, International Building
611 Gravier Street
New Orleans, Louisiana 70130
501 527-5070

Maine State Commission on the
   Arts and Humanities

Richard D. Collins
Executive Director
State House
Augusta, Maine 04330
207 289-2724

Maryland Arts Council

James Backas
Executive Director
15 West Mulberry Street
Baltimore, Maryland 21201
301 685-7410

Massachusetts Council on the Arts
   and Humanities

Louise G. Tate
Executive Director
14 Beacon Street
Boston, Massachusetts 02108
617 727-3668

Michigan Council for the Arts

E. Ray Scott
Executive Director
10125 East Jefferson
Detroit, Michigan 48214
313 222-1090

Minnesota State Arts Council

Dean A. Myhr
Executive Director
100 East 22nd Street
Minneapolis, Minnesota 55404
612 339-7691

Mississippi Arts Commission

Mrs. Shelby R. (Lida) Rogers
Executive Director
P. O. Box 1341
Jackson, Mississippi 39205
601 354-7336/584-6870

Missouri State Council on the Arts

Frances T. Poteet
Executive Director
Room 410, 111 South Bemiston
St. Louis, Missouri 63117
314 721-1672

Montana Arts Council

David E. Nelson
Executive Director
Room 310, Fine Arts Building
University of Montana
Missoula, Montana 59801
406 243-4883

Nebraska Arts Council

Leonard Thiessen
Executive Secretary
P. O. Box 1536
Omaha, Nebraska 68101
402 345-2542

Nevada State Council on the Arts

Merle L. Snider, Chairman and
    Acting Director
124 West Taylor Street
P. O. Box 208
Reno, Nevada 89504
702 323-2116

New Hampshire Commission on
    the Arts

John G. Coe
Executive Director
Phoenix Hall
North Main Street
Concord, New Hampshire 03301
603 271-2789

New Jersey State Council on the
    Arts

Byron Kelly
Executive Director
27 West State Street
Trenton, New Jersey 08625
609 292-6130

New Mexico Arts Commission

Mrs. Katie Ely, Secretary
Lew Wallace Building
State Capitol
Santa Fe, New Mexico 87501
505 827-2159

New York State Council on the
    Arts

Eric Larrabee
Executive Director
250 West 57th Street
New York, New York 10019
212 JU6-2040

North Carolina Arts Council

Edgar B. Marston, III
Executive Director
State of North Carolina
Department of Art, Culture and
    History
Raleigh, North Carolina 27611
919 829-7897

North Dakota Council on the Arts and Humanities

John Hove, Chairman
North Dakota State University
Fargo, North Dakota 58102
701 237-7143

Ohio Arts Council

Donald R. Streibig
Executive Director
Room 2840, 50 W. Broad Street
Columbus, Ohio 43215
614 469-2613

Oklahoma Arts and Humanities Council

Donald W. Dillon
Executive Director
Suite 410, 1140 N.W. 63rd
Oklahoma City, Oklahoma 73116
40 521-2931/843-1385

Oregon Arts Commission

Terry R. Melton
Executive Secretary
494 State Street
Salem, Oregon 97301
503 378-3625

Commonwealth of Pennsylvania Council on the Arts

Robert Bernat
Executive Director
503 North Front Street
Harrisburg, Pennsylvania 17101
717 787-6883

Rhode Island State Council on the Arts

Ann Vermel
Executive Director
4365 Post Road
East Greenwich, Rhode Island 02818
401 884-6410

South Carolina Arts Commission

Wesley O. Brustad
Executive Director
Room 202-A, 1001 Main Street
Columbia, South Carolina 29201
803 758-3442

South Dakota State Fine Arts Council

Charlotte Carver
Executive Director
108 West 11th Street
Sioux Falls, South Dakota 57102
605 336-8050, Ext. 650

Tennessee Arts Commission

Norman Worrell
Executive Director
Room 222, Capitol Hill Building
Nashville, Tennessee 37219
615 741-1701

Texas Commission on the Arts and Humanities

Maurice D. Coats
Executive Director
403 East Sixth Street
Austin, Texas 78701
512 472-8237

Utah State Institute of Fine Arts

Wilburn C. West
Executive Director
609 East South Temple Street
Salt Lake City, Utah 84102
801 328-5895

Vermont Council on the Arts

Frank G. Hensel
Executive Director
136 State Street
Montpelier, Vermont 05602
802 828-3291

Virginia Commission on the Arts
  and Humanities

Frank R. Dunham
Executive Director
Rm. 932, 9th Street Office Bldg.
Richmond, Virginia 23219
703 770-4493

Washington State Arts
  Commission

James L. Haseltine
Executive Director
4800 Capitol Boulevard
Olympia, Washington 98504
206 753-3860

West Virginia Arts and
  Humanities Council

Ewell Cornett
Executive Director
State Office Building No. 6
1900 Washington Street East
Charleston, West Virginia 25305
304 348-3711

Wisconsin Arts Council

Oscar Louik
Executive Director
P. O. Box 3356
Madison, Wisconsin 53704
608 266-0190

Wyoming Council on the Arts

Ms. Susie Blair
Acting Executive Director
P. O. Box 3033
Casper, Wyoming 82601
307 265-5434/234-8782

TERRITORIES — ARTS
COUNCILS

American Samoa Arts Council

Mrs. John M. Haydon, Chairman
Government House
Pago-Pago, American Samoa

Guam—Insular Arts Council

Louise Hotaling
Director—University of Guam
Box EK
Agana, Guam 96910

(local representative)
A. B. Won Pat
200 Maryland Avenue, N.E.
Washington, D.C. 20242
202 963-4655

Institute of Puerto Rican Culture
(Instituto de Cultura Puertor-
riquena)

Ricardo E. Alegria
Executive Director
Apartado Postal 4184
San Juan, Puerto Rico 00905
809 723-2115

Virgin Islands Council on the Arts

Stephen J. Bostic
Executive Director
Caravelle Arcade
Christiansted, St. Croix
U.S.V.I., 00820
809 773-3075, Ext. 1

CANADA
Provincial Arts Council

Alberta

Walter Kaasa
Director, Cultural Development
Government of Alberta
504 Financial Building
Edmonton, Alberta

British Columbia

The Chairman
British Columbia Cultural Fund
Parliament Buildings
Victoria, British Columbia,
Canada

Manitoba

Mary Elizabeth Bayer
Executive Director
Manitoba Arts Council
Room 114, 555 Main Street
Winnipeg, Manitoba

New Brunswick

Allan Crimmins
Director of Handicrafts
Office of Cultural Affairs
Office of the Premier
Fredericton, New Brunswick

Newfoundland

John C. Perlin
Director of Cultural Affairs
Newfoundland Arts and Culture
Centre
Department of Provincial Affairs
P. O. Box 1854
St. John's, Newfoundland

Nova Scotia

Mr. Allison Bishop
Supervisor
General & Specialist Services
Continuing Education Program
P. O. Box 2147
Halifax, Nova Scotia

Ontario

Louis Applebaum
Executive Director
Province of Ontario Council for
the Arts
151 Bloor Street West
Toronto M5S 1T6 Ontario
416 961-1660

Prince Edward Island

Frank Storey
General Manager
Confederation Centre
P. O. Box 848
Charlottetown, Prince Edward
Island

Quebec

Guy Frégault
Sous Ministre
Ministere des Affaires Culturelles
Hotel de Gouvernement
Quebec 4, Quebec

Saskatchewan
Vern E. Bell
Executive Director
Saskatchewan Arts Board
200 Lakeshore Drive
Regina, Saskatchewan, Canada
   S4S 0A4

Appendix VIII:

STATE EXTENSION SERVICES OF THE UNITED
STATES DEPARTMENT OF AGRICULTURE
(For further information on Craft Fairs, etc.)

ALABAMA

Auburn University
Auburn, Alabama 36830
(205) 826-4444

ALASKA

University of Alaska
College, Alaska 99701
(907) 479-7259

ARIZONA

University of Arizona
Tucson, Arizona 85721
(602) 884-2711

ARKANSAS

P.O. Box 391
Little Rock, Arkansas 72203
(501) 376-6301

CALIFORNIA

University of California
2200 University Ave.
Berkeley, California 94720
(415) 642-7252

COLORADO

Colorado State University
Fort Collins, Colorado 80521
(301) 491-6281

CONNECTICUT

University of Connecticut
Storrs, Connecticut 06268
(203) 429-3311, Ext. 238

DELAWARE

University of Delaware
Newark, Delaware 19711
(302) 738-2504

DISTRICT OF COLUMBIA

Federal City College
1424 K St., N.W.
Washington, D.C. 20006
(202) 638-4726

FLORIDA

University of Florida
Gainesville, Florida 32601
(904) 392-1761

GEORGIA

University of Georgia
Athens, Georgia 30601
(404) 542-3824

HAWAII

University of Hawaii
Honolulu, Hawaii 96822
(808) 944-8234

IDAHO

University of Idaho
Moscow, Idaho 83843
(208) 885-6151

ILLINOIS

University of Illinois
Urbana, Illinois 61801
(217) 333-2660

INDIANA

Purdue University
Lafayette, Indiana 47901
(317) 749-2413

IOWA

Iowa State University
Ames, Iowa 50010
(515) 294-4576

KANSAS

Kansas State University
Manhattan, Kansas 66502
(913) 532-5820

KENTUCKY

University of Kentucky
Lexington, Kentucky 40506
(606) 257-4772

LOUISIANA

Louisiana State University
Baton Rouge, Louisiana 70803
(504) 343-7444

MAINE

University of Maine
Orono, Maine 04473
(207) 581-7200

MARYLAND

University of Maryland
College Park, Maryland 20742
(301) 454-3742

MASSACHUSETTS

University of Massachusetts
Amherst, Massachusetts 01002
(413) 545-2766

MICHIGAN

Michigan State University
East Lansing, Michigan 48823
(517) 355-2308

MINNESOTA

University of Minnesota
St. Paul, Minnesota 55101
(612) 373-1223

MISSISSIPPI

Mississippi State University
State College, Mississippi 39762
(601) 325-4436

MISSOURI

University of Missouri
309 University Hall
Columbia, Missouri 65201
(314) 449-8186

MONTANA

Montana State University
Bozeman, Montana 59715
(406) 587-3121, Ext. 271

NEBRASKA

University of Nebraska
Lincoln, Nebraska 68503
(402) 472-7211, Ext. 2966

NEVADA

University of Nevada
Reno, Nevada 89507
(702) 784-6611

NEW HAMPSHIRE

University of New Hampshire
Taylor Hall
Durham, New Hampshire 03824
(603) 862-1520

NEW JERSEY

Rutgers—The State University
P.O. Box 231
New Brunswick, New Jersey 08903
(201) 247-1766, Ext. 1306

NEW MEXICO

New Mexico State University
Las Cruces, New Mexico 88001
(505) 646-1806

NEW YORK

New York State College of
  Agriculture
Ithaca, New York 14850
(607) 256-2117

NORTH CAROLINA

North Carolina State University
Raleigh, North Carolina 27607
(919) 755-2812

NORTH DAKOTA

North Dakota State University
Fargo, North Dakota 58102
(701) 237-8944

OHIO

Ohio State University
2120 Fyffe Road
Columbus, Ohio 43210
(614) 422-6891

OKLAHOMA

Oklahoma State University
Stillwater, Oklahoma 74074
(405) 372-6211, Ext. 212

OREGON

Oregon State University
Corvallis, Oregon 97331
(503) 754-2713

PENNSYLVANIA

Pennsylvania State University
University Park, Pennsylvania
   16802
(814) 865-2541

PUERTO RICO

University of Puerto Rico
Rio Piedras, Puerto Rico 00928
(809) 765-8000

RHODE ISLAND

University of Rhode Island
Kingston, Rhode Island 02881
(401) 792-2476

SOUTH CAROLINA

Clemson University
Clemson, South Carolina 29631
(803) 656-3382

SOUTH DAKOTA

South Dakota State University
Brookings, South Dakota 57006
(605) 688-4147

TENNESSEE

University of Tennessee
P.O. Box 1071
Knoxville, Tennessee 37901
(615) 974-7114

TEXAS

Texas A. & M. University
College Station, Texas 77843
(713) 845-6411, Ext. 40

UTAH

Utah State University
Logan, Utah 84321
(801) 752-4100, Ext. 268

VERMONT

University of Vermont
Burlington, Vermont 05401
(802) 656-2990

VIRGINIA

Virginia Polytechnic Institute
Blacksburg, Virginia 24601
(703) 552-6705

VIRGIN ISLANDS

P.O. Box 166
Kingshill
St. Croix, Virgin Islands 00850
(809) 773-0246

WASHINGTON

Washington State University
Pullman, Washington 99163
(509) 335-7205

WEST VIRGINIA

294 Coliseum
West Virginia University
Morgantown, West Virginia 26505
(304) 293-5691

WISCONSIN

University of Wisconsin
432 North Lake St.
Madison, Wisconsin 53706
(608) 262-3786

WYOMING

University of Wyoming
University Station
Box 3354
Laramie, Wyoming 82070
(307) 766-3253

Appendix IX:

OTHER SOURCES FOR REFERENCE MATERIALS FOR CRAFT FAIRS, ETC.

Mr. William R. Seymour
Craft Specialist
United States Department of
   Agriculture
Washington, D.C. 20250

American Crafts Council
44 West 53rd Street
New York, New York 10019

Appendix X:

SOURCES FOR INFORMATION ON MAIL ORDER
REGULATIONS AND BUSINESS PRACTICES

For Information on Mail Order
Regulations, Write:

United States Department of the
Treasury
15th Street & Pennsylvania Avenue N.W.
Washington, D.C. 20220

For General Mail Order Trade
Information, Write:

Associated Third Class Mail Users
1725 K Street N.W.
Washington, D.C. 20006

Direct Mail Advertisers Association
230 Park Avenue
New York, New York 10017

Mail Order Association of America
612 N. Michigan Avenue
Chicago, Illinois 60611

INDEX

ABOUT THE AUTHOR . . .

LETA W. CLARK has worked professionally both in clothing design and in marketing and promotion. Soon after graduating from Pembroke College, she joined the promotion staff of The Lurex Yarn Division of the Dow Chemical Company. In 1958, she began a small business designing beach and sportswear and later joined the design staff of Peter Pan International as a consultant. In 1967, she returned to promotion working for Metlon Metallic Yarns and in 1968 became Director of Marketing for the Mohair Council of America. Currently, she is teaching a seminar entitled *How To Market Your Crafts* at the New School for Social Research in New York City.